Health Care Benefits Problem Solver for Human Resource Professionals and Managers

Health Care Benefits Problem Solver for Human Resource Professionals and Managers

CHARLOTTE McDANIEL, Ph.D., R.N.

John Wiley & Sons, Inc.
New York • Chichester • Brisbane • Toronto • Singapore

Library of Congress Cataloging-in-Publication Data:

McDaniel, Charlotte Jane.
    Health care benefits problem solver for human resource professionals and managers / Charlotte McDaniel.
        p. cm.
    Includes bibliographical references.
    ISBN 0-471-00658-0 (cloth)
    1. Insurance, Health. 2. Employee fringe benefits. I. Title.
HD7101.M32 1994
658.3'254—dc20   93-36894
                                                                      CIP

Printed in the United States of America

10 9 8 7 6 5 4 3 2 1

Dedication

To Kris and Kirk who encouraged me
with pride and good humor

Acknowledgments

The development of a book is surely the synthesis of many contributions and experiences. This list only partially acknowledges the many persons who have influenced my thinking and assisted in shaping my philosophy and approach to health care. To them I offer my appreciation and acknowledgment.

More particular to this book, I want to thank the people with whom I talked during the development of the manuscript. To some of them I owe a word of appreciation for a case or the suggestion of a problem requiring a solution. To others I am in their debt for contributing problems or issues facing health care benefits directors. In alphabetical order they include Tom Aageson, Larry Cotrell, Mike Giliotti, Liz Keonig, Gary Matsen, and Carolyn Nilson. My editor, Mike Hamilton, was most supportive as was his editorial staff. To them I also want to express my appreciation.

To my family and friends I owe gratitude for their encouragement and enthusiasm for this work and for their support and inquiries during the preparation of this manuscript.

Preface

The director of human resources holds a unique, yet, challenging position. The pivotal role of the director is basic to this book. Our economic climate and health care reform create an environment of change. Change offers administrators opportunities to create a tailored program for workers. It offers the opportunity to provide incentives for productive work. It provides the opportunity to enhance relationships between employers and employees. Change offers opportunity to address the health—not the illness—of American workers. These opportunities are, indeed, important challenges for the future of American firms. Use this book as a resource to assist in designing and meeting those challenges.

This book is organized around problems and solutions using a logical planning approach. The author assumes directors will revise their company's current health care benefits program. Thus the underlying philosophy of this book—its problems and solutions—is analyzing, planning, and forecasting in order to remain competitive. This approach is critical for the benefits program as well as for the company and its employees. With this underlying philosophy in mind, the problems of and solutions to today's and tomorrow's benefits programs for health care are presented.

The first three chapters focus on benefits analysis. Chapter

1 provides solutions to problems administrators face in assessing the company's current program. Assessments form the basis of designing a new or revised program. The second chapter addresses the problems and solutions as possibilities for change are explored. As administrators cut health care benefits, the third chapter offers solutions to problems among employees and companies when cutting occurs.

Chapters 4 through 11 are designed to address specific categories of problems to assist in planning programs. Chapter 4 is specific; it explores solutions to particular employee dilemmas. Attention is turned to employees with ability challenges, those who want family leaves, or employees with high risks or job stress. In keeping with the focus on managed competition, Chapter 5 highlights problems and solutions posed by managed care and changes in health service delivery. Relevant to these are problems emerging with shifts away from illness to health and prevention; also communicating change to employees. Chapter 6 presents problems directors face with increasing emphasis on flexible approaches.

In Chapter 7 strategies for retaining employees through health care benefits are presented. Rewarding employees for their work vis-à-vis health care benefits is explored in Chapter 8. These two chapters highlight the importance of health care benefits for employees and the role of the administrator in tailoring their benefits. Chapter 9 focuses on policies, regulations, and federal guidelines, emphasizing new or recently developed ones. For that reason, the family leave bill and new retirement regulations receive more attention than others. The increasing use of part-time and temporary workers in America is the basis for Chapter 10. New regulations relating to retirement as well as the expanding population projected for older and retired workers are considered in Chapter 11.

The last two chapters address prevention and forecasting phases of benefits administration. Prevention phases, explored in Chapter 12, are central to the director's role. Solutions to problems that encourage directors to forecast and design a program relevant in the twenty-first century form the basis of solutions to problems in Chapter 13.

This book serves as a guide to anticipating and preventing problems before they occur, as well as assisting with the resolution of ones that inevitably do. By focusing on problems as well as solutions, directors of human resources can tailor a health care benefits program to enhance companies and employees. This book enhances the role of the benefits director by providing solutions and strategies that will be relevant to the administration of benefits well into the next century.

The author has made every attempt to provide the reader with accurate and timely information, however, the reader is encouraged to check the most current sources before making any changes based solely on this material.

Contents

1

Assessing Your Company

Among the important decisions a director of human resources makes regarding health care benefits, no decision could be any more important than assessing the direction of benefit resources for the company. Assessment provides a foundation for decisions regarding cuts, planning, and directions for benefits. This chapter introduces a number of questions that directors will encounter as they move through the process of examining their own business, assessing where to go, then whether to cut and, if so, what to cut among health care benefits. In addition, it will explore strategies for moving through this process and emerging on the other side of decision making in a manner that is positive for the director, for the company, and for the employees. Although this process of assessing in order to determine what the next step should be takes time, it is well worth the investment. Astute assessments save dollars and enhance the motivation and productivity of your company's employees.

DETERMINING WHAT TO CUT

Q How do I know what to cut?

A Assessing your company to determine what to cut involves

1

an assessment of your employees. Get a complete list of all claims in the past five years and organize them according to the size of claim with the largest as the first or highest. Then, examine what the largest amounts are. It would also be helpful to link amounts with employees, as you may have some costly employees in your company.

Q Do we need to cut?

A Cutting is an individual company determination. However, in these days of cost containment and high technology one of the largest outlays of any company is health care. While your company may, indeed, not need to cut it is hard to imagine that that would be the case. An assessment will assist you in determining if you need to cut. Last year, about 20 percent of the outlay of an average company was paid for employee health care costs (Thompson 1992, pp. 16–20).

Q We want to continue health care insurance but we are a relatively small company and are not sure where we stand. Given there are few norms, how much does the average small company spend on health insurance for its average employee?

A This is a good question since it gives you some ballpark figures for comparison. In a recent year, the average spent per employee in national companies was $3,573 (Thompson 1992, p. 16).

Q Is there an indication health care costs are increasing, and if so, how much?

A Figures in 1991 found there was a 13 percent increase in the cost of employer medical payments (Gannett News Service 1993). Such costs should lead to a rash of new plans.

Q   Is there a list of items I should consider or run through in order to make a decision about cuts?

A   There is no formal list but the following are important to consider. Tailor them in terms of "weight" for your own company, employees, or situation. Consider the size of the company in terms of product distribution, type of product, number of employees, budget size, environment in which your company is based, available options, and what you currently are offering. These are fundamental.

Q   I am not sure what the environment has to do with cuts. What does one look for in terms of the environment?

A   The environment can be discussed in terms of several features. First is the current national environment for health care which is somewhat turbulent. Second is the more immediate environment in which your company is based, and third, how your company thinks of itself in terms of an "environment." For example, if your company product is an international one, then the environment is quite different and more complex than a company with a regional product or a more defined parameter for distribution. In these instances your environment is easier to assess and predict in terms of health care.

Q   How can the environment influence the company?

A   If the environment is turbulent, it is complex, erratic, and difficult to assess; it changes quickly and dramatically. This influences both your employees as well as the benefits and profits of your company.

Q   How will this affect our employees?

A   Those employees who work in what is termed a turbulent environment may feel that they are on shaky ground and want features offering stability. Thus, they may look for stability in their benefits in ways employees in other companies, or in other environments, would not.

Q   What impact will health care benefits cuts have on our company?

A   The influence of the cuts will be determined largely by how the company goes through the process of both determining the cuts as well as the implementation of the cuts. However, in most instances, health care cuts will influence American business.

Q   How does the size of the company affect health care benefits?

A   The larger the company the more readily the company can absorb large claims or offer more options on a benefits menu. The smaller company, usually under 100 employees on a steady payroll, may have to limit its offering.

Q   Should I use the term *cuts*?

A   Why not? Everyone else is. Perhaps *cutbacks* or *reductions* are more palatable terms. Nevertheless, most people know that a term like reduction is another way of saying cuts. Call it what it is and use candor as a means of enhancing your image as a person of integrity with your employees.

Q   What impact will health care benefits cuts have on our employees?

A   The impact on employees will depend both on how much you cut and what your company specifically decides to cut. The process of cutting can be as important as the actual cut itself. Read on for more information on specific issues related to managing reductions. In fact, the metaphor for today's health care environment could be termed "managing reductions."

Q How much advance notice should I give to employees regarding cuts?

A To some extent timing is determined by the size of the company and the amount of time communication travels within your organization. About a week is the average, give or take some days. Because employees are poised for news when they return to work on a Monday, a document released on Monday will be distributed throughout the company by Friday, but one released on a Wednesday will take longer. If the cuts involve loss of key coverage allow at least a month of advance notice to give employees enough time to make a realistic alternative plan.

Q How can I determine our most costly benefits?

A Start by listing all the benefits you offer, placing first those you suspect will be the most frequently claimed, or those of large financial amounts even if for a one- or two-time claim. Then, get copies of last year's claims. You can then do one of two things contingent on the size of your company. If you work in a large company randomly select about a dozen claimants. List all claims and place those amounts in the list by the company claim list. Or, for a smaller company, list all of them. A computer is helpful in keeping track of these claims as well.

Q How do we compare to the big picture?

A One assumes that the big picture is the large well-functioning company. The average company today spends more than $3,000 on health care per employee annually, whereas, a smaller company spends, on average, more than $3,500 per employee annually. The real question is how much of your gross product you spend on health care, not actual dollar amounts (Thompson 1993, p. 38).

Q   What is the bottom line on health care benefits and cuts?

A   The bottom line is that your company does not want to spend more than 20 percent of its gross company product on health care benefits. In fact, in terms of future projections, it would be wise to come in at less than that amount. The essential bottom line is the balance between paying out for employees and the productivity of your work force in terms of their return. Only you, as the human resource director, can determine if there is an appropriate balance.

Q   We need to compare our company costs with those of other companies. We think we are out of line but we do not know. Where can we get such information?

A   Sources vary. However, in 1991 in all industries, benefits as a proportion of payroll were 38.2 percent with an annual cost per employee of $13,126. In manufacturing, the percentage was a similar 38.8 percent and $14,317 (Thompson 1993, p. 38).

Q   How can we get data we need into the information machine*?

A   Keep minutes and file them for future brainstorming and creative-thinking sessions. Develop some quality circles† on benefits and the future. Companies in the Northwest are doing so with great success.

---

*The information machine is a concept used to refer to the analysis and creative thinking needed for decision making in companies.
†Quality circles are discussion groups composed of key individuals designed to elicit creative thinking about critical issues.

Q   As I begin to examine areas to assess for cutting and for making changes, what are some key questions to keep in mind?

A   Essential to your assessment is your company bottom line. Among those relevant to the health care benefits sector are the questions pertaining to the insuring firm as well. For example, how stable is the company; does it increase its premiums, and how often; are the deductible rates competitive with other companies? This is information that a director would want to have prior to finalizing a plan.

Q   I keep hearing a lot about health assessments. Is this term being used today in the same way as it was used in the past?

A   Most health assessments are discussed in one of two ways, although there certainly are others as well. First is the health assessment that a patient or consumer receives to determine overall health status. That is fairly traditional, and is the way in which the concept was used in the past. However, given the current reform attention to prevention, outcomes, and community, the more current emphasis is on health assessment conducted for the community to determine what works and what doesn't (Sherer 1993, p. 36). You might use the analogy of the community for your employees and assess what works and what does not, as well as assessing and designing a plan for the future. One implication is that assessments take on broader parameters than just one patient.

Q   What are the implications for our own assessment for benefits in health care?

A   As communities assess what is appropriate for them, and design services in collaboration with medical services in response to the assessment, the results will determine what is available in health benefits plans. A proactive approach is to sit at the table with the designers, so your employees who are also community residents have a representative say in the final outcome.

Q Are there examples of community health assessments that seem to be going well?

A One example that is cited as a model is the Crozer-Keystone Health System in Media, PA (Sherer 1993, p. 36). Their integrated assessment resulted in a series of programs addressing everything from sexually transmitted diseases, infant mortality, cancer, cardiovascular illnesses, and community education.

Q How does one go about getting involved in the assessment?

A Begin with an assessment of your own health care benefits needs. Then ask about what is happening in your local area regarding community health assessment. Convey the fact that you have X number of employees—consumers—whom you represent, and ask to be involved. Services are now more receptive to consumer input than ever before.

Q These assessments seem expensive. Are they?

A A full community assessment is expensive. Cost estimates range from the informal, which is not as expensive, to a full formal assessment with professional guidance or consultants, which is estimated on the average to range from $10,000 to $25,000 (Sherer 1993, p. 38). However, Crozer's final cost of $300,000 was beyond this—very expensive.

Q Given the fact that these community assessments can be quite expensive, as illustrated by the previously described situation with Crozer-Keystone, is there any way to contain such costs?

A   Yes. One way is to set a dollar limit; another is to set parameters around the amount of time allotted to the assessment or on the number of variables (i.e., the issues or concepts) that you want to evaluate. Remember that in a community assessment no company can evaluate everything. Pick the issues or variables that are most directly related to your situation.

Q   If we assessed some needs that our employees had could that become part of a community health assessment?

A   Absolutely. For example, in New Hampshire, following a large-scale assessment, priorities were determined for providers, as well as target areas, action strategies, and short- and long-term goals and planning (Sherer 1993, p. 36). Benefits administrators of major companies in an area should have input into these target areas.

Q   Will the size of the firm influence the final outcome?

A   I would think so. A large firm with numerous employees in a focused region has a larger impact than a smaller firm, or a firm of any size with a relatively dispersed work force over a diverse area. It would be more difficult to be responsive to the latter.

Q   In terms of assessing for our health care benefits, when we examine the communities where our employees live as well as work and their resources, what is the bottom line on these community health care service assessments?

A   The key, according to surveys, is to have a synthesis of the data so conclusions can be drawn and changes can be made (Sherer 1993, p. 36). Also important is to assign a person to gather, organize, and analyze the information.

Q   In terms of assessing for change, is it true that the language is changing as well?

A   Yes and no. There will always be new terms to learn. The current ones emerge out of the managed care or managed competition phenomenon. Learn the new terms so you can negotiate competitively with your insurers. Several of the new terms are interchangeable and if used in the correct context, may get you a better price. Many of the old terms are still in use, however.

Q   I am trying to learn the new language, which seems very complex, but I find that the insurers never have the same term for the various features in their packages. Is this just my reading of the situation?

A   Not at all. A number of benefits analysts would agree with you. Some insurers give their packages unusual names to identify the insurance package with their company or to suggest uniqueness.

Q   What is a good strategy to begin to assess the policies that I may need to examine in determining cuts?

A   Turn on the computer, create a table, and enter the relevant comparative data. At the top or the side place the key points which you want to compare: costs and premiums, increase rates, deductibles, what is covered, insurer stability, drug coverage, life insurance, and company history for canceling policies. These are only a few suggested features to compare but you can tailor your table to your company. Then, you have a table of data that can be updated, and, better yet, shared with your boss or with your employees.

Q   What are the major categories I need to examine in terms of assessing where we go from here?

A   That will vary a bit with individual companies, and with the demographics of the employee pool. However, here are a few suggestions: overall medical coverage, hospital coverage, miscellaneous coverage such as pregnancy, preexisting conditions, and supplemental group insurance. These are fairly standard issues across firms.

Q   We are examining the possibility of including dental coverage. How popular is this item in the average firm's health benefits package?

A   In 1940 and 1960 reports dental coverage was not available for reporting as an item. However, by 1980, 80,528,000 persons were covered in the U.S. (Harrington 1985). As a comparison, during the same time period, hospital expenses went from $11,962,000 to $198,000,000.

Q   What is the most comprehensive coverage?

A   In general, the Medicare coverage in Part A is the most comprehensive (Harrington 1985). However, it may change in the future with the increasing attention being given to health maintenance organizations (HMOs).

Q   In terms of dollars and cents, just how much do companies pay out as an insurer to the employees for health insurance?

A   In the 1980s, for example, companies like the Blue Shield and Cross plans reported a total of $88,210,000,000 paid out; the amount represents an average of an 80 percent payout (Harrington 1985, p. 3).

Q   What was paid in by the company?

A   Again, during the 1980s, there was about $111,186,000,000 paid in premiums for health insurance in the U.S. as a means of providing insurance to prevent employees from risk and the need to pay health services expenses out-of-pocket (Harrington 1985).

Q I understand in terms of assessing where we ought to go we should think in terms of the Three Cs. What are the Three Cs?

A There are a number of variables to assess in determining where your firm ought to move, but the Three Cs provide a good place to start. The *Three Cs* stand for competition, capitation, and collaboration (Cerne 1993, p. 50). These three are reshaping the health care market of today and will continue to do so.

Q Is it true that collaboration is involved in the system? It seems today's emphasis is on competition, not collaboration.

A You are an astute observer of the contemporary health care system. Nevertheless, there is a growing collaboration, perhaps stemming from the acknowledgement that the competition inherent in the health care system can be costly. For example, a model developed in Portland, OR uses a collaborative approach among several facilities which share the expense and the use of one lithotripter (Cerne 1993, p. 50). Such collaborative ventures will become more common.

Q If collaboration is the byword for this new era of health care, would it not be prudent for employers such as us to get into the act? How can we be more involved?

A This is an excellent question, and one to consider for the future. For starters, consider more collaboration between your company and the primary insurer you select or currently use. For example, you might team-up on educational endeavors, share personnel resources that are relevant to both of you, or offer a company program such as immunizations for employee dependents that can reduce insurance costs by enhancing prevention. Although any potential conflict of interest should be avoided, these collaborative endeavors can contribute to your company's overall cost savings.

Q In terms of enhancing the collaboration regarding new models of health care, is it true that there is more emphasis on information and sharing of information?

A Yes, but it is a complex situation. Success stories like those found in Oregon, for example, suggest that it is best to develop the information system as one develops the model of care. However, companies may be able to take advantage of these currently evolving information systems to enhance the benefits program.

Q We understand there is more discussion among providers regarding continuum of care. What is the focus of this dialogue?

A The focus is on successful provision of continuity of care, called continuum of care. Analysis of success stories suggests that taking the former hospital model, for example, and applying it to nonhospital services like those in the community, will not be successful in the long run. New models are proposed. Explore these in detail for your company.

Q We think the continuum of care for our employees is very important. Are there features we should examine as we begin an assessment of our company for planning and creating change?

A A good place to start is with the following list based on a company success story. The list includes the following six variables: costs, care management, the relationships among the physicians and between them and other providers, the services and sites, the structure of the administration, and the management of information (Lumsdon 1993, p. 28).

Q It seems everyone is focusing on the cost containment dimension of the health care business, or is it just the interest of industry? Is there a trend toward diversity?

A Yes. The trend extends beyond business, or, for that matter, the national agenda. There is a world emphasis noted in recent reports from the World Bank. The emphasis is on diversity in services and regulation as well as the familiar emphasis on cost effectiveness and those services helping the disadvantaged (Passell 1993, p. C2).

Q If world emphasis is the case, what are the implications for assessing a company in today's turbulent health care market?

A That is a good question. The suggestion is the emphasis will be on efficiency, cost containment, and competition such as that found in care managed systems (Passell 1993, p. C2). In addition, put into your company's plan some means of determining the health care outcomes, as research is a byword for today. Data to assist with assessment will be important to your company.

Q What are the most common ways of thinking about health insurance? We need to rethink what we do.

A Even though you may change your benefits package, there are still only several ways of categorizing it in today's market. As health maintenance organizations become increasingly common in benefits packages, the following four-part approach is most often used. The broad categories are major medical, physicians, surgical, and hospital expenses (Enteen 1992). These categories cover most eventualities.

Q In addition to these, are there others? What are they?

A Other approaches are looking at major medical, a base plan for hospitalization, and for medical and surgical coverage (Enteen 1992, p. 5). These are similar to other categories but with different divisions. Use the categories that best fit your company program.

Q What are some of the more common factors employers can use to determine where to go with the changes in benefits?

A Although the changes are significant and may be even more dramatic in the future, there are still several basic questions. Those suggested are the needs of your particular employees, including their demographics and the risks of injury in terms of the work or products of your company. The needs of the company also must be considered. These, placed in a balance, should guide you in assessing for future change.

Q In terms of assessing our firm and what we might do, several of our older employees have suggested we explore the long-term insurance market. What is the general opinion of long-term policies?

A Long-term insurance options as a benefit gained in popularity because they are needed, and the demand is increasing. They are noted, however, as a "proceed at your own risk" category in terms of an offering.

Q Is it true most companies have more than a dozen days of restricted activity due to illness? We want to know where we stand because we have more than that amount.

A While you do not say how much more illness your company has, the average in the late 1980s was about 15 days per year per employee for both acute and chronic conditions (Lumsdon 1993, p. 28).

Q Is it true as we assess our company's health care we should pay particular attention to the expenses of the elderly?

A Probably. The elderly accounted for 44 percent of the expenditures for personal health care but only 12 percent of the total population in the same year (Lumsdon 1993, p. 28).

Q In terms of an assessment, it would be wise to consider the next five to ten years. However, health care is changing so rapidly I am not sure a ten-year projection is realistic. Is that true?

A No one needs to tell you the health care climate in the U.S. at this time is volatile. You are absolutely correct to be concerned about very long range projections. Nevertheless, a five-year plan is realistic, as is a ten year plan based on flexible projections. The retirement projections for liability, for example, involve one type of benefit assessment needing to be projected in a flexible manner.

CONSIDERING STRATEGIES FOR IMPLEMENTING CUTS

Q What about an association? As a small company we have considered an association but we are not sure about its merit.

A   These plans are popular since they provide the opportunity for companies that are small to become members of a pool. The group as a whole, the pool, then has more clout to negotiate for desirable coverage (Thompson 1992, p. 16).

Q   As a small company we are concerned about our high-risk employees and wondered what options might be possible. Would an association program meet that need?

A   Since the association pools resources it also has the advantage of dispersing the high-risk employees, or coverage, across the members of the pool. To this end, then, it is certainly an advantage for a smaller company that might otherwise need to drop such a costly employee's coverage.

Q   Are there different types of plans within an association? If so, what are they?

A   According to research there are two main types of association plans (Thompson 1992, p. 19). The first is the self-insured plan members pay into and from which the claims are collected as premiums. The second type is the insured plan which is purchased from a commercial insurance company.

Q   We know our benefits have increased in costs but have everyone else's?

A   Absolutely, which is why there is such an emphasis on reducing costs. It will get worse. For example, surveys found that in 1991, employee benefits needed an extra $0.39 of coverage. The cost represents an increase of 5.8 percent over the prior year (Thompson 1993, p. 38).

Q   We want a way to assess the better HMOs; how can we do that?

A There are services officially rating programs and services including HMOs. One, based in Atlanta, provides rates and services in a booklet called *HMO Buyer's Guide* (*Money* 1993, p. 110).

Q Our company wants to develop a way for our employees who are health care consumers to rate what they think is good care. How can we do an employee rating?

A Set up an advisory board composed of the service recipients and discuss the issues that are of concern to the company.

Q I understand a phenomenon called subacute care is developing at a rapid pace. What is this and should we consider it for an assessment?

A Yes. *Subacute care* is the transition between traditional acute care in hospitals and nursing home care. It is designed for those patients who are still quite ill but need longer stays than those currently allowed under the Diagnostic Related Group (DRG) system. These subacute patients are those who would not do well in a typical nursing home (Taylor 1993a, p. 58). This transitional phase is relatively new to health care delivery and has emerged following the limited hospital stays introduced with DRGs.

Q How should we assess for this emerging type of unit and its care?

A One would expect plans in the future will reimburse for these services mainly because they are less expensive than the acute-care services. Since one driving force for the development of subacute units is the aging population, it may be a significant force in retirement packages for health care benefits. Put this type of care into the computation for retirement health care but at a less costly amount than acute care (Taylor 1993, p. 58).

Q   What are other strategies we should consider as we assess for cuts?

A   You probably have a plan in place less focused on outpatient care—on transitional care, or on ambulatory care. There are also others but these forms of services will clearly increase in frequency and attractiveness in the future. Plan now to provide for them since they will, overall, be less expensive than traditional inpatient services.

Q   What about the educational components of a health care benefits plan?

A   Few plans are well designed in the current environment to account for the educational features that parallel the emerging emphasis on prevention. Plan these into your package and consider offering them on-site to get what you want.

Q   Why should we consider offering educational programs on-site in contrast to purchasing them?

A   You can always arrange a purchase of educational offerings. However, there are secondary gains to be considered like the enhanced relationships between management and employees, the *esprit de corps* or more group cohesion for teams of workers. These can be built into the prevention and health promotions programming. If it is on-site you can control it to a greater degree than if it is off-site.

Q   As we assess for change, as a cost reduction strategy we are thinking of aligning with more urgent care centers, but our current plan does not cover these. Is this a wise move?

A   Yes. Based on projections for the next century, of the services currently offered in hospitals—either in-house or outpatient—about 35 percent of the procedures are projected to move to urgent care centers* (Data Watch 1993, p. 52).

Q   What about imaging procedures? We hear they, too, may move out.

A   Along with a number of hospital-based procedures, imaging centers† are projected to account for more than 35 percent in the move to alternative settings (Data Watch 1993, p. 52).

Q   Do these types of services (illustrated by urgent care and imaging centers) represent a trend? What should we expect?

A   Yes. They represent a trend in the continuing change from inpatient services to outpatient services. The number and range of services predicted to be offered in the nonhospital setting—in communities or similar nonhospital sites—is expected to expand.

Q   Among the services predicted to increase in outpatient or community settings, which ones are predicted to change the most?

A   Preventive medical counseling is predicted to increase in volume by 87 percent, followed by such services as developmental testing (55 percent), mammography (35 percent), and MRIs (magnetic resonance imaging) (34 percent) (Data Watch 1993, p. 52).

---

*Urgent care centers are community-based facilities offering modified emergency care.
†Imaging centers offer imaging services located in community settings.

Q   What are some of the changes and strategies we can anticipate and plan for in terms of responding to the emphasis on
outcomes?

A   More data on the outcomes, behaviors, and quality of life of
employees. Plan and assess now for a way to build evaluation into your benefits package. It will assist you to predict,
to determine if you are getting the best service for your
money, as well as knowing what to eliminate or reduce.

Q   Are other settings doing outcome evaluations?

A   Yes. For instance, there is a new Center for Outcomes
Research built into the educational department of the St.
Vincent Medical Center in Portland, OR (Taylor 1993b, p.
43). Since hospitals and other health care services are moving
in this direction quite rapidly, companies are anticipated to
do so in the immediate future.

Q   We have a number of milling firms with sites located in
rural areas in several states. One worker is married to a
professional nurse who told him about a health insurance
purchasing cooperative (HIPC). What is a "hip-pic" and is
it a relevant strategy?

A   *HIPCs* are relatively new and responsive to health reform.
The term, which refers to health insurance purchasing co-
operatives, was coined by Prof. Alain Enthoven, one of the
key planners in health care reform. Rural states, like those
in which your companies are based, are using HIPCs to
achieve a modified form of managed competition and reduce costs while providing services. The HIPC achieves
universal coverage with provider networks that are exclu-
sive (Blankenau 1993, p. 34).

Q How will these HIPCs affect benefits for employers?

A The jury is still out on the precise nature of all reform, but if HIPCs include only the smaller employers, those with under 100 workers, then the larger firms will need to address a managed competition form of service to stay cost-effective for their own companies.

Q What about our workers?

A One role of the HIPCs is to assist the worker in selecting a good plan—one with quality and efficiency.

Q Are an alliance and a HIPC essentially the same?

A Yes. Both are forms of cooperative arrangements with some nuances. Each provides a network or group of insurers from which services are purchased.

Q Won't these be increasingly limited under health care reform?

A While the federal government sets parameters for health networks, it will be unlikely to set an exact number and form for them (Blankenau 1993, p. 34). As they evolve the parameters will become clearer.

Q We are fearful that larger firms will not be included in the HIPCs of the next century. Is this true?

A It is too soon to tell. However, there have been discussions about limiting the companies HIPCs would serve (Blankenau 1993, p. 34). The cutoff is pending, but 100 employees is the most frequent marker point (or benchmark amount).

Q   As a firm we are continuing to assess what to offer well into the twenty-first century. Are there states like ours—we are in Florida—that are moving in the direction of HIPCs?

A   Yes. In addition to Florida, Vermont, Washington, Minnesota, and California are also exploring coverage under the HIPC model. Keep in touch with their benefits administrators to see how it evolves because the models in those states are promising.

STRATEGIES FOR DAMAGE CONTROL

Q   How can I survive as a human resource director?

A   By making your boss happy with the plans you initiate and by treating your employees fairly in a direct and honest manner. The writing is on the wall with respect to health care cuts, and employees know this. You are implementing some national initiatives. Tell them, and your boss, that.

Q   Will employees blame me?

A   Of course they will. You know as well as any other human resource director that every company has at least one employee who will blame someone or anyone. You, as the human resource director, will get blamed, especially if you deliver the bad news. Accept that. Then do what you can to diffuse it. You might even tell your employees you expect it, but tell them why it is not realistic. Essentially, cutting is not your decision. Your decision is what and how much to cut and how it is handled. In this way you can come out a good guy.

Q   As an administrator for benefits, it seems to me I am inundated with questions from my employees. Are others getting the same thing?

A   Yes. There are several reasons for this trend, particularly the current national climate. However, it is buffeted by the increasing emphasis on joint decision making among health care consumers. It will increase, not decrease.

Q   How can we assess and plan for this?

A   Go proactive. Offer seminars, information, and publications, and let the workers know you have the information or the resources to inform them. It can be a good preventive strategy.

Q   What are the buzz words that go with this phenomenon?

A   The most common in the current medical literature is patient partners or partnerships referring to patient, physicians, and registered nurses.

Q   My employees tell me they are scared. What can I tell them?

A   You cannot control what reaction an employee has to pending news or even to their projected idea about pending news. However, you can reassure the employees your company is a concerned company, is interested in its work force, and will do what it can to create a realistic package for the company and its employees. Nevertheless, this is one area where you might garner some employee support by getting them more involved.

Q   What will I tell my employees about health care cuts?

A   What you tell your employees will depend on what phase you are in regarding planned cuts and how much and what you need to cut. It you are in the initial planning phase, then you tell them nothing. However, if you are near to an announcement and know cuts are inevitable, then tell them a package will be announced shortly.

REFERENCES

Blankenau, R. 1993. Designing HIPCs. *Hospitals & Health Networks*, 20 July: 34.

Cerne, F. 1993. Networking: Portland, Oregon. *Hospitals & Health Networks*, 20 June: 50.

Data Watch. 1993. Outpatient procedures. *Hospitals & Health Networks*, 20 July: 52.

Doctor network. 1993. *Money* 22(7): 110–13.

Enteen, R. 1992. *Health Insurance*. New York: Paragon House.

Gannett News Service. 1993. Surviving in a health care jungle. *New York Times*, May: 1.

Harrington, G. 1985. *The Health Insurance Fact & Answer Book*. New York: Harper & Row.

Lumsdon, K. 1993. Exploring the continuum of care. *Hospitals & Health Networks*, 5 July: 28–30.

Passell, P. 1993. Economic scene. *New York Times*, 8 July: C2.

Sherer, J. 1993. Health assessment. *Hospitals & Health Networks*, 20 July: 36.

Taylor, K. 1993a. Poised for growth: Subacute care gains a clearer identity. *Hospitals & Health Networks*, 20 July: 58.

Taylor, K. 1993b. Shopping for surgery. *Hospitals & Health Networks*, 20 July: 43.

Thompson, R. 1992. How to buy health insurance. *Nation's Business*, October: 16–20.

Thompson, R. 1993. Benefits update: Benefits costs surge again. *Nation's Business*, February: 38.

2

Exploring for Possible Change

Every director of human resources wants to know what options are available in his or her area. What are the possibilities prior to embarking on a change? This chapter highlights a number of possibilities in health care delivery which can influence the decision for a final health care benefits plan and related changes. This chapter provides an overview of a number of creative possibilities, again providing challenging questions with their solutions.

Q   We would like to know more about what possibilities are out there. What, for example, is a health maintenance organization?

A   A *health maintenance organization* (HMO) is a form of managed care which emphasizes a preventive approach. Physicians are paid on a salary basis as opposed to a fee-for-service basis. The consumer generally receives all of his or her health care in this facility, including any annual checkups. There are some exceptions, for example, major surgery. Consumers pay a premium.

Q What are MSOs?

A In a *management services organization* (MSO), network participants form a separate entity providing an administrative service to physician practices. The focus of MSOs is on management, not the service aspect of health care. Often, an MSO is used to coordinate the contracts for managed care; it allows different groups to practice together. The owners can be HMOs, physicians, hospitals, or even entrepreneurs (Hudson 1993, p. 31).

Q What is meant by an integrated system?

A Usually, in terms of health services, an integrated system is one in which an original entity like a hospital purchases or affiliates with another system; they integrate and thereby are larger than the original service. There are two major forms of integration, vertical and horizontal.

Q Would an integrated system be advantageous for our employees?

A It depends on the type of system. An integrated system can often provide a broader range and depth of services not available in smaller or single service organizations. Also, since the services are essentially provided from one integrated system there may be less cost involved.

Q I see a lot of new models out there. What are the ones that seem to be most popular and have a chance of surviving all the turmoil?

A It is always difficult to predict accurately the survival of models. There are several that seem quite viable. The three, according to reports (Hudson 1993, p. 31), are the fully integrated facility, the management services organization, and the medical foundation. Remember these models are concerned with the legal dimensions of the service model and not the delivery of care.

Q Among legal models is there one that physicians seem to prefer?

A There are advantages and disadvantages to all three: Physicians like the MSO because of its versatility and because they can assist in how this model is run. While physicians may have a say in the decisions regarding MSO systems, MSOs do have liabilities.

Q At a recent meeting I heard about joint ventures that differ from the traditional collaboration between companies to enhance their benefits package. What is being done?

A A number of formats are being developed to assist firms in reducing costs. One way is for two different companies to form a network to reduce costs (Lumsdon 1993, p. 34). According to a recent report, the network has about 50 primary care physicians and the services are paid for according to a fee schedule with utilization monitored by a board plan composed of physicians and employers. This form of network saves all the participants money with annual increases capped at 5 to 7 percent.

Q What are flexible benefits?

A Flexible refers to a choice employees have in selection of benefits they want. The choice may be influenced by the employee's age or by other coverage options they have. For instance, a young person with less emphasis on retirement may elect child care, whereas a married male with no other coverage may choose family coverage.

Q What are cafeteria plans?

A A *cafeteria plan* is a form of flexible plan. In essence it is a concept borrowed from the food service industry whereby the benefits features are chosen as one would choose menu items. The cafeteria plan offers the employees a number of options. An added feature of cafeteria plans is if employees pick wisely—in line with employer preferences—they receive a reward (Harrington 1985). Such rewards are usually in the form of cash bonuses or cash savings. Today, some companies are exploring the option of a company stock reward.

Q Can you given me an example of how a cafeteria plan would work in terms of its reward system?

A There are several success stories. For example, using the generic spectrum of drugs, or opting for a higher copayment or deductible on the part of the employee saves the employer money. The savings can be returned in various proportions to the employee.

Q What should we include in our cafeteria plans?

A The types of benefits to include will depend on what you wish to retain as a benefits package, your projection of what it will cost your company, and your employee profile. As a human resource director, you need to determine a picture for your company.

Q How can we manage a change to a cafeteria plan?

A The question is how can you manage an inevitable change well so your boss, you, and your company and employees come out with a sense you are working together to be productive. Health care benefits are aimed at keeping employees well, healthy, and on the work force. Cafeteria plans enhance employee choice which motivates employees to accept inevitable change.

Q   We need to improve our image while we are cutting health care benefits. How can we do this?

A   This is an opportune time to enhance your company's image while cutting. You, as a human resource director, know that most companies are cutting or at minimum making reductions in some areas. Use this information to link your company more tightly with employees, especially in the current work environment where employees sense they might be dispensable. One key way is to get your employees involved in some of the assessment phases.

Q   How can I involve employees in the assessment?

A   The first decision is what decision, if any, you want employees to make. Then, if you want information from them, solicit it. Conduct a survey in which you find out how they feel about cuts. What are their ideas of the most important benefits? Or, use employee focus groups, or representative groups of employees, if you want to target specific issues like retirement.

Q   We need to begin to make changes in our health care benefits. Where do we start?

A   Obtain all claim forms from your employees over the past ten years. Categorize them into major areas such as chronic, acute, or size of claim. Then obtain an average of these for your employees. See if there is a relationship between the claim and the length of employment, type of employment, or other demographic categories (like sex, age, number of dependents, etc.). Once you have this information, you have a foundation upon which to begin to make your final decisions.

Q We would like to change health care benefits coverage but the options in our relatively small town are not numerous. What should we do?

A Get information from the nearest academic health science center to see if they would be willing to contract for coverage on a container basis. Some providers are willing to travel to a site if there is enough demand and time can be efficiently used.

Q I am relatively new in my position as the director of human resources in a midsize company. However, health care changes loom on the horizon and we need to make adjustments. We do not know as a company what employees would prefer. What should I do?

A Print up a professional-looking survey, short and specific. Ask the employees to rate their preference being sure to indicate that this data will be compiled along with others. Response rate will be high if you indicate this data are a part of the final assessment for what is possible. Put on the survey list only those items your company can offer, or include several you would be willing to explore. You want to avoid implying a promise based on these responses alone. Assess these employee responses, and compare them with preferences from national surveys. Take into account what are realistic options for your company.

Q We conducted a survey of employees to get information about their preferences as we attempted to decide what was possible regarding health care coverage. The data was not conclusive. What do we do now, if anything?

A   Follow up on the survey with focus group discussions over lunch or on a work break. Use these sessions to problem shoot unclear or problematic areas. Again, state clearly that these discussions are for information and not for final decisions (unless, of course, they are).

Q   Would a committee work?

A   Yes, perhaps a committee of key employees in the company could represent several employee sectors and meet with you at the assessment phase to determine which benefits to reduce or eliminate, and which to keep and in what amount. Be careful not to ask employees for information or suggest decisions in areas in which they cannot make that decision. That can lead to antagonism in the long run.

Q   Are some health care benefits more desirable than others?

A   Yes, just as some are more costly than others. This desirability will be linked to your employee work force, and to which items have been widely used by the force, and those which are of long standing. The latter is, to some extent, tradition. Desirability will also be related to possible use if there are no other options for some employees.

Q   Can we use our benefits package to project what we want?

A   Yes, and you should. You want a healthy, productive work force. By rewarding employees you can pull them along to that objective. Reward good health as well as daily work attendance.

Q   How can we balance employees' preferred health care benefits with our company's preferred list?

A   You need to assess and compare both your employees'

preferred list with your company's preferred list. Start with a list of what the company wants. Then conduct a survey, or form a focus group to determine what it is the employees want. You might find out an expensive offering is not a high priority for the majority of employees. You can use this data both in cutting as well as in developing a sound rationale for why you cut in that area. This will assist you in dealing with the inevitable one employee who wants that item kept!

Q   Can employee health care benefits ultimately be budget neutral?

A   While budget neutrality would be an ideal situation most companies do not find it possible. Nevertheless, careful planning, cost analysis, and employee assessment can give you data on which to tailor a package coming very close to budget neutral.

Q   We are a medium-size company in a large metropolitan area. Thus, we sit in a highly competitive environment. How can we enhance our competitive edge vis-à-vis health care benefits?

A   Use your health care benefits package to attract and retain employees. One edge would be to assess what your competition is offering, then offer a different or more attractive package. If you tailor your package to the work force you have, you will retain workers in a competitive manner. However, it obviously will not work to offer an item that your employees do not value or that would unbalance your fiscal bottom line. You need to be realistic about your company and the environment in which it is based. Attend to tailoring and implementation of what the company decides to offer.

Q   We need to change from a focus on illness or cure to one of health and prevention. How can we begin to make that change?

A   Start with all conversations you have with your employees, with tagging information on bulletin boards, and finally with the items you delete and retain in your benefits package.

Q   Do we need to keep all our current health care benefits?

A   The question cannot be answered until you do a company assessment. However, it would be unusual to keep all the current benefits since you would need to offer more drastic reductions in them. If you actually cut some out, then you can offer minimum increases in the amount of copayment needed on the part of the employee or smaller deductible increases for your employees.

Q   What are the most important health care benefits for employees?

A   To determine the answer to this question you need to conduct an assessment of all your employees. You can do this in several ways. Use prior claims, or go directly to the employees to get information, or both.

Q   What benefits are used the most?

A   The most-claimed benefits are reflected in your claims statements and can be used to assess for data to answer this question. Go back through your claims and categorize the top five or the top ten, according to the frequency and amount of claim. To address the question of which are used the most you want those most frequently claimed. However, this may not be the question: It may be the employees want the one used the most, that is, the most frequently claimed, but the company needs to know which was the most costly category—the most expensive. You are in an excellent situation if the most frequent is less expensive and is not the most costly. Offer it to your employees.

Q How can I determine which benefits to keep and which to drop?

A You will need to have an idea from your boss of the amount or the percentage of your company revenue allocated to benefits. Then, you need to assess the company output in this claim area and determine those used the most frequently and those not used. The equation of those valued by your company should be a melding of those that keep your employees at work and do not create a large company financial outlay, balanced or set against those valued by the employees of your company and actually claimed in a given time, perhaps last year. If last year was an unusual year either because it was too costly or not reflective of other time spans, go back for three or five years or randomly select claims to assess over the past five years.

Q We need some suggestions about strategies to cut costs. What are other firms doing?

A Strategies vary, but many are taking quite assertive approaches in cutting costs. Some of the options companies are frequently exploring are increased emphasis on the managed-care models, like the health maintenance organizations (HMOs), more use of utilization reviews, increased deductibles and cost-sharing by employees, and more rewards for healthy employees (Gannett News Service 1993, p. 1).

Q We have real differences between our industry and the local community in which we operate. We must cut health care benefits, but one of our employees is the chair of a local consumer board. What can be done to appease this person?

A Create a committee of "concerned consumers as employees" and have them meet with you to discuss health care benefits and the projected influence on the local community. Include in this mix or committee a local physician or nurse practitioner who is liked and respected in the community. In addition, get the local United Way executive director and the director of an organization like the Rotary Club on your committee. In other words, create a valid link between your company and your community. This might be called the "Health Care Advisory Board" or a similar name. Keeping the term advisory makes it clear they offer advice to you but they do not make the final decision.

Q We need to increase our employee amount of deductible. How do I decide what rate to use?

A Find out what rates are being used by competitive companies similar to yours. Assess this amount in terms of where you are at this time. If the gap is great, then a phase-in is warranted or you will create more dissension with a sudden radical increase.

Q We are rethinking our self-insurance, and as a small company we anticipate we may drop it. What are other companies doing? How do we compare with other small national companies?

A According to surveys categorizing companies by size, among small companies with less than 100 employees, about 43 percent are offering self-insurance at this time (Thompson 1993, p. 24).

Q What about companies that are larger? How do they compare on self-insurance?

A For companies with more than 500 employees, 15.1 percent are using self-insurance (Thompson 1993, p. 24).

Q What are the advantages of a self-insurance plan in contrast to other types?

A Companies may escape the state tax on insurance premiums and it exempts them from the benefits laws mandated by most states. In addition, there is increased control over the plan format by the employer. These are three key advantages but there are others for an individual company (Thompson 1993, p. 24).

Q What is the essence of a flexible benefits plan?

A To pay health insurance premiums, flexible benefits plans allow an employee to set aside his or her pretax dollars for their own payment and reimbursement of those payments not covered by insurance.

Q If we want to follow national trends in changes, where is the big growth?

A According to the Group Health Association of America (Thompson 1993, p. 24), the health maintenance organization (HMO) increased the most in recent enrollment figures. In their annual survey, over 18 percent of all employees are insured under this type of plan with increases predicted.

HEALTH MAINTENANCE ORGANIZATIONS

Q What is predicted to be the large growth area in the future to plan for now?

A   National enrollment in the health maintenance type of organization (HMO) appears to have the edge in overall growth. Surveys note an increase of 41.4 million subscribers in 1992, up from an earlier enrollment of 2.8 million (Thompson 1993, p. 24).

Q   We want to know what the most cost-effective forms of insurance for benefits are. What is the cost efficiency of an HMO compared to other types of plans currently being offered?

A   According to surveys, the HMO types of plans are quite cost-effective. For example, in the last year HMOs cost $3,313 per employee per year compared to other forms, which averaged $4,080 per employee (Thompson 1993, p. 24).

Q   We are a small firm with several subsidiaries in other small cities and communities. We work very closely with local Chamber of Commerce organizations in those communities. Do they have a position on the current benefits changes, and if so, what is it?

A   As you can imagine, the Chamber of Commerce is not going to endorse any particular type of plan, however, they have indicated support for the managed-competition approach (Thompson 1993, p. 24).

Q   Are there particular issues regarding health care benefits with which civic organizations in communities are concerned?

A   Yes. The United States Chamber of Commerce, the national organization of Chambers of Commerce, has stated several areas for which it would have strong opposition. Among others the key features include elimination of self-insurance, plans excluding lower-wage workers, federal price controls, focus on the private sector, and elimination of costly packages (Thompson 1993, p. 24).

HMOs AND QUALITY CARE

Q Recently, a good employee with a strong track record came in to talk with me about the proposed changes in health care benefits. She knows we are considering the possibility of shifting to a health maintenance organization (HMO). Her concern is if we shift to an HMO it would not offer employees quality treatment or good physicians; she thinks HMOs offer care of lesser quality. Although I am sympathetic to her situation, I am not sure she is correct. Is she?

A It is probable that your employee is accurate in some cases, but certainly not all. In fact, data suggest the opposite. The efficiency and quality ratings on HMOs are quite high when one examines survey results (Hudson 1993, p. 31). Talk with her about her specific concerns.

Q Are there other data to substantiate that HMOs are a viable possibility?

A Yes. In reports on the number of HMOs hiring board-certified physicians, which is a strong indicator of provider quality, the numbers are high. Board certification is as high as 70 percent among network medical staffs, a very high proportion (Hudson 1993, p. 31).

Q What exactly is board certification?

A Once a medical doctor has completed the initial training in medical school—usually four years—then he or she must also complete a year of internship and then a residency. A board-certified physician is one who has completed seven to eight years in a residency specialty like surgery or dermatology. In addition, they must also pass a rigorous written–oral examination.

Q Are there a lot of board-certified physicians in the U.S.?

A Board certification is an advanced step for physician training. In the U.S., 48 percent of medical doctors are board certified (Thompson 1993, p. 24).

Q Is there an organization that actually rates plans?

A Yes. For your own detailed information, the HealthPlan Management Service, which is based in Atlanta, GA, does an annual survey on best networks. Their annual results can be obtained by writing to them (Thompson 1993, p. 24).

Q I understand some firms are starting to offer benefits to same-sex partners. Will we be required to offer these benefits as well? We are a small firm of about 35 employees and are afraid it would increase our benefits beyond what we can manage.

A It is true according to recent news reports that several companies are implementing this option (Noble 1993, p. 1). Companies are not required to offer this benefit, however.

Q We are interested in obtaining data-based information on various policies so we can compare the prices. Are there companies that provide this service?

A Yes, there are several that do what you are asking. Three are reported in a recent article: Dinan (New Almaden, CA), Quotesmith (Palatine, IL), and Signal Data (Chattanooga,

TN) (Thompson 1992, p. 18). This listing does not endorse them, but simply lets you know such services are available.

Q If our office wants to obtain a computer software program that would assist us in analyzing the data in our health benefits office, could we get such a program? For example, it would be helpful to put into a program the information we want to explore in terms of our benefits package—like a deductible range and the maximum for a family to pay out. Then we could see what is a feasible amount for our firm to offer.

A Such programs are coming onto the market and more are anticipated in the near future. *Nation's Business* noted several offering those facilities: Quotesmith is one, and also Signal Data and Dinan.

Q I want a detailed analysis for benefits of several health insurance policies we are exploring. Where could I get such information?

A Companies that offer benefits analyses are commonly in computer-programming businesses which focus on health care policies. Several are on the market—with more planned—and should be listed in your public library reference section.

Q Last week I had to meet with our insurance firm to discuss a number of issues. However, I felt overwhelmed by the amount of information that I needed to determine which insurance premium is best. Even then, it may be a shot in the dark. How can I best make a final decision?

A It is always helpful to attend such meetings with your own data prepared ahead of time. Several companies will, for a modest fee, provide you with comparative analyses of the various benefits and their insurers. Having this data before you attend your next meeting will help. Three noted recently in articles are Signal Data for companies with up to 50 employees, Dinan particularly for small businesses, and Quotesmith. Fees range from $15 to $59 (Thompson 1992, p. 18).

Q   As we begin to rethink our coverage I am hearing a lot about loss ratio. What is a loss ratio?

A   The loss ratio is the proportion of payments a company pays for its coverage; a good company has a high loss ratio, say above 90 percent. A company with a loss ratio of 60 percent is quite low, given Blue Shield and Blue Cross nonprofit systems have a ratio ranging between 90 and 95 percent. A loss ratio is a gauge on company quality.

Q   I am told there are four keys to the reform movement. What are they and do they influence benefits?

A   Within the managed-competition framework there are four central foci with differing emphases and details: standard benefits package, tax reform, health plans, and HIPCs (Kotelchuck 1993, p. 4).

Q   Am I right that most benefits administrators like to think of benefits as benefits-as-need, that is, they are developed out of the employee's need, in contrast to an approach in which the employer focuses the benefits, perhaps to target a group or as an incentive? How will this approach influence what I communicate to our employees?

A   There are two main philosophies of health care benefits, the benefits-as-need approach and the benefits-as-added-compensation (Foster 1986). If the main emphasis of the company is a need approach usually the form of communication is quite direct. The information regarding benefits is clearly and explicitly conveyed to workers in communications through newsletters or other communications put out by the benefits office.

Q What about the benefits-as-added-compensation approach? How would that information be communicated?

A When the latter is the main approach, then the benefits administrator usually conveys not only factual information but additional data pointing out the advantages and the disadvantages of each component. The benefits program under this philosophy is more integrated into a relationship between the company and the worker.

Q Although, in general, our benefits and health care are always undergoing reforms, under the newer approaches will health care benefits administrators have as much flexibility as in the past?

A The answer will depend on company size. Among the smaller firms, those with less than 100 workers, they may move into more directly managed benefits programs. The larger firms will have as much flexibility if not more to purchase from alliances, competitive arrangements, and other integrated or network services. Flexibility does remain, but costs are projected to go down.

Q We know we will change our benefits program but we want to keep a positive image in our local community. Will retaining our positive image be possible?

A I would think so. In the final analysis changes affecting your firm will also affect others, contingent upon size and location. Otherwise, it is a matter of how you handle the changes rather than what they actually are. Consider becoming proactive in the management of these changes.

Q Our company is based in an area where there are a lot of retirees, including some of our own former employees. The impression benefits administrators get is that many retirees do not want to make decisions about benefits. They simply want to be offered a package and then directed from there. Is this typical of this age group?

A Yes and no. There is a tendency on the part of some people to not want to make many decisions, some related to age and others totally unrelated to age. However, you need to plan according to your community. Perhaps in the past there were fewer options, so choice was less of an issue. In any event, this situation places more emphasis on the communication between your office and your retired employees.

Q We think a strategy to enhance our possible choices and be proactive in anticipation of major changes would be to go into the community and hold discussions with a number of our retirees. Our firm is located in an area where a number of our former employees live and some have family members currently on our payroll. Does this seem like a feasible way to consolidate our efforts to manage image control and deal with change?

A Sounds like a creative proactive way to address the issues. A logical place to start is with local community groups: the Rotary, Kiwanis, or Chamber of Commerce clubs in your various communities. You could branch out from there. Let us know how it works!

Q My CEO thinks we should be offering some financial planning for the administrators in our large company. However, I don't see how we can do so when things are in such flux. What do you think?

A These are cautionary times, and thus your decisions must depend on the purpose. If it frees up management time then it may be well worth the cost and effort. Even so, if the consultant is on commission, given the turbulence in the field, it might be wise to wait. A good compromise would be for the benefits office to sponsor an executive seminar over a nice dinner. During dessert provide a question and answer session.

Q Will the job of the benefits administrator change dramatically with the onslaught of the reform changes?

A A lot depends on what finally happens. However, the costs should be reduced, paperwork should be reduced, and the overall package may be more manageable in terms of the health care dimension. Again, much depends on company size and the number of employees. The one area of continuing perplexity is the retirement portion with increased liability factors.

Q What or when are the key times we should initiate some communication with our employees regarding benefits?

A There are several which you probably have used for an individual employee, but here is a relatively complete list. Begin with the moment you have new employees join the firm, and, of course when they terminate or retire; when cutbacks are announced; when changes are made; or corporate changes affect benefits (Foster 1986). These are the key opportunities, although there may be others for an individual firm.

REFERENCES

Foster, R. 1986. *The Manager's Guide to Employee Benefits.* New York: Facts on File.

Gannett News Service. 1993. Surviving in a health care jungle. *New York Times*, May: 1.

Harrington, G. 1985. *The Health Insurance Fact & Answer Book.* New York: Harper & Row.

Hudson, T. 1993. Three major models. *Hospitals & Health Networks*, 20 June: 31.

Lumsdon, K. 1993. A formula for shoes, plywood, and primary care in Arkansas. *Hospitals & Health Networks.* 5 June: 34–37.

Kotelchuck, R. 1993. Managed competition: A guide to the thicket. *Health Policy Advisory Center* 32, Spring: 4.

Noble, B. 1993. HBO grants benefits to staff's same-sex partners. *New York Times*, June: 1.

Thompson, R. 1992. How to buy health insurance. *Nation's Business*, October: 18.

Thompson, R. 1993. Health-reform watch. *Nation's Business*, July: 24–27.

3

Cutting Back on Health Care Coverage

One of the most difficult decisions facing the human resource director is the reduction of health care benefits. Not only is it inherently difficult, but the nuances of what to cut, where to cut, and how much to cut are more complex than many other decisions required in today's company. Health care is, indeed, a complex business and knowing how to cut in a way to satisfy both the company and the employee is a professional challenge. This chapter addresses the complexity of health care reduction by discussing the possible ways in which the firm may reduce the benefits and ways to handle those cuts.

THINKING CUTS AND COLLECTING DATA

Q Our CEO stresses quality over cuts, but cut we must! What to do?

A Stay with quality if quality is what your boss and CEO want. However, attention to quality does not mean you cannot attend to cuts or reductions. Create a package reflecting your own assessment of your company needs and abilities, then tailor it tightly to those of your employees. Decisions that emanate out of an assessment like that will reflect quality cuts. Your aim is to create a tailored package for your company, a package that reflects quality reductions.

Q   As we consider cuts, just how desirable are health care benefits? In other words, does the average employee want benefits?

A   In results of a national comparison using a survey approach among employees, the three top worker satisfiers were health insurance, benefits, and job security (Caggiano 1992, p. 101).

Q   We assume we need to cut but we are not sure how much health care spending has increased. Is it true that the growth in this area is tremendous?

A   Absolutely. For example, during the years between 1948 and 1990 the spending by companies for health insurance in the private sector grew at the rate of 15.6 percent annually (Piacentini and Foley 1992).

Q   Is it true most employers are cutting back?

A   Absolutely. Recent surveys reveal employers are reducing health care benefits by as much as 25 percent (Thompson 1993, p. 38).

Q   What about elimination of benefits?

A   In 1991 there was a reduction of 2 percent in companies actually offering health care benefits (Thompson 1993, p. 38).

Q What perception do employees have of companies that cut?

A Start with how your employees currently view your company. Do any employees perceive your company as an unconcerned company? Does your company take action to counter a negative image? If you find negative images are prevalent among more than just a few workers you need to pay attention to this information. Create a plan to counter the negative image on behalf of your company. And let your boss know you are implementing such a plan!

Q What is the difference between managed care and managed competition?

A Managed competition is a rather generic term that refers to health reform in which the foundation is a market competition among health care facilities. Managed care is more specific and refers to the type of service offered in which one practitioner will manage the care of health care consumers or patients. Both have as their basis the containment of costs, as well as an emphasis on quality.

Q Aren't all the proposed changes really the same?

A Not at all. You need to assess which are emerging as the most important and pervasive ones, and then see how they will influence your company.

Q What are the implications—subtle or not so subtle—for the bottom line?

A The implications are not subtle. Each company needs to develop a benefits plan or package to keep its company viable with a healthy work force creating a productive outcome; one that will not erode the company's bottom line. The objective is a company bottom line that is balanced, and, preferably, a benefits package that will contribute to that balance, not to the deficit. Even with tax write-offs the company needs to have a less than balanced bottom line in the company's favor since increasing future costs are projected.

Q   We want to cut and would like to know the big areas in health care benefits. Where do health care benefits fit into the big picture?

A   As a fringe benefit, after paid vacations health care is the most common.

Q   We are thinking of cutting health insurance, but it would be helpful to know how many companies offer health insurance before we go ahead with this proposed cut. What is the proportion of companies currently offering health insurance?

A   Of the 3.7 million U.S. companies in the late 1980s, 56 percent offered health insurance (EBRI 1987).

Q   We think we may cut out sick leave and reduce life insurance. How would we compare to other companies?

A   Behind the majority of other U.S. companies. Of the majority of companies with health benefits, 30 percent offer life insurance and 37 percent offer sick leave (EBRI 1987).

Q   Since we are a relatively small company, with about 50 employees, we assume that we would be in the minority if we offered a full package for health benefits. Is this true?

A   Yes. Of firms with more than 500 employees the majority offer a full(er) package with pension (EBRI 1987). The smaller the firm the smaller the package, is the rule of thumb.

Q We are concerned because as our company has grown in size, so have our benefits costs. How can we keep them down?

A There is a direct relationship between costs and size of the company: The larger the company, the larger the proportion of health care costs in company outlays (Piacentini and Foley 1992).

Q What rank, in terms of importance to employees, is health insurance?

A According to surveys conducted by the Gallup Poll in 1991 among a list of 16 desired satisfiers among U.S. workers, good health insurance and other benefits ranked at the top with a rating of very important by 81 percent of those polled. Among those responding, 27 percent are satisfied (Caggiano 1992, p. 101).

Q We are a small company in a fairly risky business because we sell liquor. How much chance is there that we will be turned down for insurance?

A Refusal will depend on your background but you are wise to ask. In a recent survey, bars and taverns were not insured by 31 percent of insurance companies. The smallest group, physicians' groups, were refused by only 6 percent (Thompson 1992, p. 16).

Q What proportion of their overall costs are the majority of large firms paying for their health care?

A Among larger firms hovering around 500 employees and above, they spend about 13 percent (Piacentini and Foley 1992).

Q What about smaller firms? What proportion do they tend to pay out?

A Smaller firms pay around 7 percent of their costs in health care benefits (Piacentini and Foley 1992).

Q We sense the larger companies in our community are being very proactive, even aggressive, in cutting costs. We are benefiting from this community image but we are not sure we can hold out. Is this typical?

A It is typical that larger companies are more active in cutting costs (Piacentini and Foley 1992), but then their overall costs are larger than smaller firms.

Q What are the most common ways used to cut costs today?

A The most common ways to cut costs are the following: about 43 percent are increasing the employee deductible; carrier change is used by 32 percent; second opinions with surgery, 31 percent; and using outpatient surgery, 25 percent (Piacentini and Foley 1992).

Q How effective have these measures been for the companies introducing these strategies?

A Of those using one or more of these measures, studies report 84 percent found them effective (Piacentini and Foley 1992).

Q Of those measures, are some more effective for smaller firms? We only have about 30 employees but our costs are skyrocketing.

A Yes. Strategy varies with size. For example, among smaller firms the increase in the size of the employee deductible was the most effective. That addresses companies with fewer than 24 employees and of those, 81 percent reported increasing the deductible as an effective strategy (Piacentini and Foley 1992).

Q   We are giving serious consideration to cutting out our dental benefits. It seems, nationally, not many companies are retaining dental care. Are we right?

A   Dental care seems to be involved in a first cut at this time. However, much depends on the ages of the companies' employees since employees near retirement and those with young children tend to have a higher priority on dental care.

Q   We have the impression we are out of line with other employers, spending an average per year of $5,000. How much, on average, does a company spend on an employee for health care?

A   On average in 1991 a company spent $3,605 on health care benefits alone, based on surveys (Piacentini and Foley 1992).

Q   Is there a great variety in what we employers offer to employees? What do most offer?

A   Based on surveys of a cross section of companies, employers tend to offer the following: physician visits, hospitalization, x-ray and lab services, and nonhospital prescription drugs (Piacentini and Foley 1992).

Q   We are thinking of drastically reducing our hospitalization coverage in order to cut back further. What would this do to our position in terms of other companies and what they offer?

A   Since hospitalization is the single most common benefit item among firms that offer health care coverage, the cut might place your company in the outer extreme ranges. Over 90 percent of companies offering health care offered this coverage.

Q   We know our health care costs have increased, but is it true that costs have tripled in the past few years?

A   The fact is that costs of providing health care coverage incurred by the employer for employees increased more than 100 percent between the years 1984 and 1991 (Piacentini and Foley 1992).

Q   We want to cut back on our employee coverage and may eliminate our family coverage entirely. However, before we do, we want to see what the averages are for monthly individual coverage among other local government employers like ours. What are those figures?

A   An average monthly premium for the individual employee, using national average statistics from 1990, is $25.53 (Piacentini and Foley 1992, pp. 262–72).

Q   Do the figures above hold true for employees of agencies operated by federal and local governments?

A   Among state and local government facilities, the average monthly premium for a family was $119.59 (Piacentini and Foley 1992).

Q   What are the comparable figures for the nongovernment employers?

A   Among smaller firms in the private sector, the monthly family and individual premiums are $109.34 and $25.13, respectively (Piacentini and Foley 1992).

Q   As we cut back, we are going to increase our annual deductible we ask employees to pay. However, we want to know if it is true the most commonly used deductible amount is $100.

A   Apparently not. As early as 1989 fewer than 5 percent of all full-time employees had an annual deductible of less than $100. The remainder had a larger one (Piacentini and Foley 1992).

Q   What is the most common deductible amount?

A   Current literature suggests that an employee amount of $250 is the most common (Thompson 1992, p. 20).

Q   Does the $250 deductible amount represent a significant change?

A   Yes. In 1980 less than 10 percent of full-time employees paid $100 in deductibles; by 1990 it was about 55 percent of full-time employees, predicted to increase beyond the more common $250 by the mid-1990s.

Q   What do these changes in the deductible represent in terms of costs?

A   In 1984 the cost per employee was $1,645 in contrast to the 1991 average of $3,605 per year (Piacentini and Foley 1992).

Q   In terms of cutting back, what are the main aims of most other companies?

A   The key aims are to reduce utilization and to limit or cut actual health care expenditures (Piacentini and Foley 1992).

COPAYMENTS AND OUT-OF-POCKET EXPENDITURES

Q As we consider cutting back, where are the greatest changes occurring?

A The most significant changes are increases in the frequency of employee contributions and the amount employees pay for their coverage. For instance, in 1984, 62 percent of employees in large and medium firms did not contribute to their individual coverage, but by 1989 this had dropped to 48 percent of all full-time employees (Piacentini and Foley 1992). The proportions keep dropping.

Q Are the percentages of employee contributions the same in small companies?

A The proportions are quite similar. For instance, among small companies, 40 percent of all full-time workers in small private companies in 1990 contributed (Piacentini and Foley 1992).

Q We are a federal agency. What are the figures for government organizations?

A Among full-time employees in local and state government organizations, those who contributed represented 57 percent (Piacentini and Foley 1992).

Q We want to be more proactive in the management of our benefits. What is the average administrative cost?

A It depends. For large and medium firms, monthly family coverage in the early 1990s was about $72.10, whereas individual coverage was about $25.31 for a monthly premium (Piacentini and Foley 1992).

Q   We are eager to cut back and contain costs. Is it accurate that employer co-insurance payments commonly reflect an amount greater than 80 percent?

A   As late as 1989 the most common amount of copayment was 80 percent for full-time employees annually (Piacentini and Foley 1992).

Q   We have a large number of employees—over 600. Do these figures apply to us?

A   Yes. The copayment amount applies to all firm sizes: small, medium, and large (Piacentini and Foley 1992).

Q   We do not currently provide an employer copayment for our employees because it is entirely too expensive for us. How popular is copayment?

A   For full-time employees, over 97 percent of employers required a copayment (Piacentini and Foley 1992).

Q   Last year we had two employees with AIDS-related illnesses. They just about wiped us out. Given the fact more and more employees seem to incur catastrophic medical expenses, we are thinking of cutting back on our out-of-pocket limit for the 300-plus employees in our firm. Where does this decision place us in terms of other companies?

A   It is an expense noted by many other companies. In 1990 slightly less than one-third of all companies had no maximum limit for out-of-pocket expenditures for employees (Piacentini and Foley 1992).

Q   My employees tell me they are scared to death of the large amounts of money health care can take. Our current limit is $1,200 dollars per year for out-of-pocket expenditures for employees. If we cut back are we saving or losing in terms of our employee relations?

A   A lot will depend on what your employees read and how much they compare with other companies. However, as a guide, in the 1990s among full-time employees, the average for the large and medium firms was between $1,000 and $1,250 (Piacentini and Foley 1992).

Q   Since we work in a number of government-related agencies we would like to see the statistics for state and local governments. What are they?

A   The annual out-of-pocket limits for the local and state governments in the 1990s ranged between $500 and $750 (Piacentini and Foley 1992).

Q   We will probably cut back on our expenses in health care by reducing the amount of our lifetime coverage. What would be a realistic cut? We currently have a limit of $1.5 million per employee.

A $1.5 million is a generous amount. Studies suggest the national average limit in 1989 was around $1 million; about 40 percent of all full-time employees had a similar limit (Piacentini and Foley 1992).

Q   Do most employers use a lifetime limit?

A   Absolutely, and the numbers are growing. Seventy-nine percent of employers who offered coverage in large and medium-sized firms in the private sector had a limit (Piacentini and Foley 1992).

Q   We are a local government agency with only a few employees at our own site. Although we will need to do what other similar government agencies do, we would like to get a sense of what is happening nationally. What are the percentages of companies making cuts in this area?

A The government represents a type of organization with the largest percentage offering a lifetime limit. For example, among both local and state government agencies, excluding the federal, more than 80 percent had a specified lifetime limit for an individual full-time employee among those participating in health care offerings (Piacentini and Foley 1992).

Q We have only 24 employees. What do most smaller businesses do? We want to be in competition with other smaller firms in our metropolitan region, but we would also like to cut back.

A Smaller firms had a slightly lower percentage—73 percent— than the larger firms. This is still a large proportion with a lifetime limit (Piacentini and Foley 1992).

STRATEGIES FOR CUTTING BACK

Q We are considering some options to reduce costs, but my CEO is skeptical that an HMO will save money. What data is available to substantiate an HMO is cost-effective?

A Information and surveys vary. However, most find an HMO is more cost-effective than fee-for-service models of care since cost containment is one of the primary aims of an HMO. For example, in a survey of consumers regarding their satisfaction as well as cost reduction, the cost of the HMO—measured in costs associated with the length of stay which is a criterion variable—was 4.1 days with the HMO and 4.8 with the national averages for comparable situations. Those days translate into a sizable cost saving over time (McNamee 1993, p. 114).

Q   Is there an increase in the number of enrollers in HMOs?

A   Indeed there is. The anticipated change reflected by surveys is up from the 1987 28.6 million enrollers to a present 45 million (Flynn 1993, p. 95).

Q   Are there other indicators of cost savings with HMOs?

A   A Northeast HMO reported a revenue increase of 23 percent last year with a 22 percent increase in enrollment (Flynn 1993, p. 95).

Q   How can I keep current and learn about evolving reform?

A   Health care reform is rapidly unfolding and will continue to do so for this decade. Keep informed with current books like this one, and follow the news. The important issues are ways in which reform will influence your company.

Q   An employee who smokes said to me, "Well, I guess I'll have to stop smoking if we are going to cut benefits." What do I say?

A   As the human resource director you are essentially in charge of health. For that reason, smile and say, "Sure, why not?" Since smoking is linked to cancer and heart difficulties why not stop now? If you really want employees to stop smoking, or to develop more healthy habits, reward them!

Q   I know that a number of employees smoke. What can I do to decrease the smoking?

A   As another or second step, ask employees what it would take to get them to stop smoking. They undoubtedly have heard about some project or program linking benefits with smoking cessation or they assume your company will insist employees stop smoking. Find out what employees know or think they know and where they obtained the information. Maybe they are candidates for an employee committee on what to offer in a company package.

Q A senior employee came in to talk with me regarding the possibility of health care cuts. She says her husband is losing his health care benefits. She wants to know what we can do for him. What can I tell her now?

A Ask if she has a specific concern in terms of coverage. For example, does her husband have a health care problem or is there a family history of a major disease? What you can tell her now depends, of course, on what you are planning and assessing for your company's package. If the company's coverage can retain a benefit addressing their needs discuss it with her. Use the information as part of the data on planning. If you have not conducted an employee survey, tell her you will take these notes but when the survey comes out to be sure to complete it and return it. Data are essential to you in planning and projecting a good package reflective of most employees' concerns.

Q There are changes pending in our health care benefits which have not been announced to our employees. One of my employees needs major elective surgery. Should I encourage her to go ahead?

A If she is planning on having this surgery, and you know this item will be cut, it would be to her advantage for you to encourage her to have it. While you cannot make the decision for her, you can tell her honestly that you are not sure at this time what is going to be covered in the future, and that it would be prudent to get any work completed while she can. Remind her that the decision is hers, however.

Q As a relatively small company we cannot offer a lot of options in health care benefits. What are the current trends for containment strategies in offerings?

A The most popular strategy for employers, according to a recent survey, is to ask employees to assume a larger proportion of the deductible. Seventy-three percent of the companies elected this route to contain benefits costs (Thompson 1993, p. 38).

Q What other routes are popular?

A The other popular option is a managed-care approach in which 78 percent of the companies used readmission certification; choice of physician was limited by 26 percent (Thompson 1993, p. 38).

Q How popular are flexible benefits plans?

A Flexible benefits plans reflect a trend among employers which is continuing. Results of a survey found that 17 percent of companies used a cafeteria benefits plan; a combination was offered by 29 percent (Thompson 1993, p. 38).

Q We are planning to purchase new insurance for health care and have heard of a strategy called pooling. What is pooling and will it work for us?

A *Pooling* is a system whereby the insurance companies place all the claims from a region or geographical area into a pool. This results in a spread of claims across a larger number and thereby stabilizes costs. It is especially useful to smaller companies or those with high claims in a year. You can find out if your insuring agent is willing to pool.

Q What does one ask to get information on insurance pooling?

A Ask your insurers if they pool. Also ask whether the company renewal is based on a group of similar businesses in an area or on the company's own individual claims background (Thompson 1992, p. 16).

Q How much can I expect to save by pooling?

A It will depend on the claims that you currently have. Recent reports, however, found by pooling claims the company reductions ranged from 9 to 15 percent for renewal increases (Thompson 1992, p. 16). The reduced percentage amount is well worth the investment in the time for an inquiry.

Q What can we do to encourage a more efficient price comparison among our employees? Surely there are ways to get our employees on board with a more prudent approach to their own copayments and benefits.

A Yes, you are absolutely right. One way suggested by a recent report is to place a limit on the amount an employer will pay. The rationale assumes that when employees have to pay more, as with a higher deductible, they will become more price conscious (Blankenau 1993, p. 31).

Q What else can we do to encourage a more prudent approach on the part of our employees?

A In addition to paying for their own health care, or at least a portion of that health care, studies suggest providing them with sound information and data is helpful (Blankenau 1993, p. 31). Financial data that indicate the actual value of their benefits may help.

Q As we move into discussions about a managed-care approach, I find a number of my employees are somewhat negative, and think this competition for management and care is not good. What can we do to foster a more positive attitude?

A As noted in several reports (Blankenau 1993, p. 31), you need to address some of the myths in health care. One of the most common myths assumes managed care is not as good; the quality is less than with previous models. You may need to have small discussion groups or follow up with a video on some aspect of managed care with a discussion and question–answer session, perhaps over lunch.

Q We want to be as proactive as possible and also to garner the support of our insurers. Any ideas as to how we can do this?

A Studies indicating the rewards of applying cost–benefit analyses find benefits analyses are increasing (Hagland 1993, p. 34). For example, in 1988 only 2.6 percent used these methods, whereas, by 1992 it was 17.6 percent, projected to increase.

Q We are a really small company without many options. We may need to completely drop our health care if we cannot think up some creative solutions to cutting back. Any ideas?

A One viable solution which is extremely cost-effective is to network with other companies or firms in your region (Cerne 1993, p. 48). One example of such a model, and one which is quite successful, occurred in Michigan where providers formed a regional health care system.

Q What are some effective ways of communicating the message to employees about their health care changes? Are there approaches that work?

A   Yes, indeed. Several companies have successfully used the following generic approaches. First, it requires effective communication. Second, address the problem from a number of angles, not just one. And, third, remember health care decisions are essentially emotional ones (Blankenau 1993, p. 31).

Q   In addition to a generic approach and attitude on the part of the company, are there some specific strategies that would help?

A   Strategies used by the Xerox Company, for example (Blankenau 1993, p. 31), include the use of surveys among employees with items on the survey indexing what employees liked most; and providing data for good decisions.

Q   We have over 300 employees. What about increasing deductibles among the larger companies?

A   Among those reported in the larger firm category, over 90 percent found increasing the deductible effective. The addition of outpatient surgery also aided in reducing costs for large companies (Piacentini and Foley 1992).

Q   Are other strategies more effective for larger firms?

A   Only larger firms report the addition of a surgical second opinion and the addition of carrier change are effective strategies (Piacentini and Foley 1992).

Q   When I attend national meetings of health benefits administrators like myself, I get the feeling that, overall, some data are weak. We cannot be too sure all these changes are really effective. Are our data sound?

A   Because several change strategies were introduced at the same time by companies, without a controlled assessment of each—either individually or in a phased approach (which adds in several items over time)—it is difficult to attribute actual effectiveness to any single specific change (Piacentini and Foley 1992, p. 31). Assess for your own company.

DISGRUNTLED EMPLOYEES

Q   As the human resource director, I know several of our employees will be quite disgruntled at the news regarding health care cuts. How can I diffuse this disgruntlement?

A   Start with the reality of the work force. On any payroll is at least one—and you are lucky if you have only one—employee who is almost always disgruntled. Treat the employee as a given and ignore the individual for the most part. Aim for a package tailoring your benefits package for the majority of the employees. Protect yourself with a package reflective of the majority of employees in your company. In order to obtain this protection, use data based in reality. Then, when the disgruntled employee confronts you, you have information you can use in a professional manner.

Q   I also know of several groups in our company that will complain about cuts. How can I stop that negative gossip before it starts?

A   Can you arrange an informal meeting with them? Or can you find a time to join them for lunch or for coffee during their group time? If not, or in combination with that strategy, place information on bulletin boards that you know they read. This information should include data and statistics on national cuts occurring in the majority of compa-nies in the U.S. It should not be hard to find an announce-ment verifying your planned change, since the majority of firms are also changing in the same direction.

Q How can I be positive in the face of delivering the message of health care benefits cuts?

A It is your attitude that matters. Be positive even if you do not feel positive. However, the package can be viewed as tailored to the company employees and can be a positive statement. There may be an offering in your current pack-age employees never use or do not value. Your question assumes you know all employees will see the cuts as nega-tive. Before you make this assumption—and certainly be-fore you act upon it—find out if the assumption is accurate or what portion of it may be. Check out your information.

Q How can I demonstrate a positive attitude while cutting back is viewed as negative?

A Your employees may see it as negative but it is part of the reality of this decade and of our current environment. Do not play into their attitude. Instead, emphasize the positive parts you and the company retain, as well as what you do for them. However, if you think that this negative attitude pervades the company and is indicative of more than just a few usually disgruntled employees, you need to see what else is going on in your company. For instance, is your company seen by the employees as cutthroat or insensitive? What is the overall atmosphere in your company these remarks reflect? What you want to avoid is the scapegoating of health care benefits when, in fact, something else may be going on in your company.

Q An employee of long standing comes into my office. He is irate his benefits will be cut and his copayment will be increased. What do I tell him?

A While you would like to tell him this is reality and to accept it, it will not work with all employees. Sit down and talk with him. The message needs to be conveyed that you understand his situation; it is true some reductions are needed since all companies are reducing. Find out what he knows, what he wants, and if there is a particular concern. Perhaps he is just anxious due to misinformation or wrong assumptions. Perhaps it has to do with his assumption about how the company will care for him as a long-standing employee. Or, is there a way to recognize long-standing and loyal employees? If so, now is the time to tell him.

Q My employees tell me they do not understand these changes. They are suspicious of secret reasons. Is this typical?

A Although this would suggest your employees are out of touch with the reality of today's work world, they do not want to hear the message. Instead, see what their major concerns are and use these data to include in your planning. These employees need some realistic information which, as the human resource director, you can provide. Make sure you have ready information about the ways cuts are coming down from other companies like yours.

Q In this era of informed consent just how much should I tell my employees?

A What you need to tell them. However, trends reflect a growing interaction between employees and employer. A partnership is the contemporary mode, rapidly replacing the manager–employee dichotomy.

Q   What can I say to employees who complain about needing to pay more on their copayment of health care benefits?

A   Health care is an increasing expense and when costs escalate they adversely affect the budget of your company. When outlay costs escalate your company has less profits, and less to pay out for salaries, bonuses, and employee benefits, including your own. Everyone is being asked to pick up more of the cost of health care.

Q   How can we plan for the future?

A   More cuts are projected into the future since health care costs are projected to increase slightly each year. For this reason, a phasing-in of cuts might be more realistic in your company. The decision will depend on where you are now with your offering and the size of the company. If you have a large company you can absorb more cuts in a shorter time; in a smaller company these reductions appear, at least, to be more drastic.

Q   What does it suggest for the future?

A   To remain viable into the next century, accurate evaluations need to be developed to measure the link between costs and strategy, especially given the increasing demand for cost containment and outcomes research.

REFERENCES

Blankenau, R. 1993. Confused consumers. *Hospitals & Health Networks*, 5 July: 31–32.

Caggiano, C. 1992. What do workers want? *INC*, November: 101.

Cerne, F. 1993. Networking. *Hospital & Health Networks*, 5 July: 48.

Employee Benefits Research Institute (EBRI). 1987. *Government Mandating of Employee Benefits*. Washington, D.C.: EBRI.

Flynn, J. 1993. The final option: Radical surgery. *Business Week*, 11 January: 95.

Hagland, M. 1993. Drug reform: A bitter pill? *Hospitals & Health Networks*, 5 July: 34–36.

McNamee, M., Weber, J., & Mitchell, R. 1993. Health care reform: It's already here. *Business Week*, 11 January: 95.

Piacentini, J., and Foley, J. 1992. *EBRI Databook on Employee Benefits, 2nd ed.* Washington, D.C.

Thompson, R. 1992. How to buy health insurance. *Nation's Business*, October: 16–20.

Thompson, R. 1993. Benefits update: Benefits costs surge again. *Nation's Business*, February: 38.

4

Challenges for Benefits Administrators

Although health care is changing dramatically, employees who have not shared in the cost of their coverage or their claims find these current changes difficult. In addition, employees who have some disability—or in current language, an ability challenge—also present challenges for the administration of health care benefits. The employees most affected by these changes are those in the lower wage categories, as well as those with physical challenges or chronic conditions. All companies are affected by the physically challenged, family leaves, job stress, and high-risk health concerns among their employees. This chapter explores a range of issues affecting changes, from a provided system to one in which employees share an increasing dollar amount of their coverage. This chapter also discusses critical common problems and offers solutions to them. Regulations and federal policies are explored, but you will find them covered in more depth and range in Chapter 9.

THE PHYSICALLY CHALLENGED

Q   Is the term *disabled* correct to use today?

A A contemporary term used by disabled groups is physically challenged.

Q Can we give more benefits to the disabled than to other employees who do not need it as badly?

A Probably not. According to the recent Americans with Disabilities Act (McKee 1993, p. 19), it is not permissible to "discriminate on the basis of a disability" for fringe benefits. See Section 1630.4.

Q Do we have to offer health care benefits to the disabled?

A No more than you would for any employees. The issue is to offer the same benefits to those with challenges as those without. Thus, the question might be, do you have to offer health care benefits, which at this time are not required.

Q Will regulations change?

A Current reforms suggest, indeed, the criteria for disability requirements may change.

Q Several of our employees are disabled. Will we get into trouble by cutting their benefits?

A As long as you treat all employees the same way, you would not be cited for discrimination. Make sure you are being fair to all employees. Unfortunately, this is one of several down sides of being an employee with special challenges who also has continuing health care benefits and reimbursement needs; the disabled, as do any other employees, take cuts as they come to all employees.

Q I was thinking of changing the medical examination we offer for our employees if they want to buy into our company-sponsored benefits program. What about the applicant who is disabled? Can we develop a medical exam that will cover the eventualities of disabled employees?

A   No. Not if you mean you want a specific examination offered to or required by those applicants or even employees who are disabled (McKee 1993, p. 22). If you provide a medical examination, it would be appropriate as a condition for employment as long as all applicants took the same exam. At issue is the offering of a special exam for disabled persons; a special exam could result in a discrimination suit against your company.

Q   If we can gather data to indicate several of our employees, including one disabled person, pose a very high risk for us in terms of providing insurance, can we get around their coverage? It is costing us a small annual fortune.

A   The laws enacted in 1992 were left vague with regard to the benefits. While one part prohibits discrimination on the basis of a disability, a later part, Section 36.212 on insurance, allows "classifying risks." Again, check thoroughly, perhaps with an attorney.

Q   We are a private company and thought private firms were exempt from the new disabilities law. Are we right?

A   Not so. There are two key subdivisions for the private companies. They are public access and employment. Check carefully so you are not targeted for noncompliance.

Q   We are a company that rarely serves the public. However, if we do begin dealing with the public, what should be our main focus regarding disability?

A   The law indicates that companies, or employers, who serve the public must make accommodation for the person with an ability challenge (McKee 1993, p. 19).

Q We are anticipating a raise in the amount employees will pay for their deductible. It may go as high as $500 per year. An employee with a physical challenge tells me he cannot pay this amount on top of all the medical bills he already has. What should I do? Is our company liable?

A If you are requiring the same deductible raise for all of your employees, or for employees in certain categories not reflecting a discrimination, then your company is not liable. Require the same deductible raise for all employees, and, according to current rulings, this will be an acceptable shift in benefits.

Q An employee has just been in my office with a concern about the pending health care benefits changes. As an employee who uses braces and a special van to get around, he is concerned changes will require him to use more time in travel from work for health care. We formerly provided it on-site and will not continue that option due to rising costs. What can I do without incurring a discrimination suit?

A If the change involves all employees there is no problem. However, in good faith, you might want to also offer employees who require a major change a phase-out which is a gradual incremental reduction of their benefits. Phasing would ease some of the anger and assist in the adjustment period.

Q In our firm we have a day-care center where caregivers are working. Are caregivers addressed under the new disability laws? What do these laws specify?

A Not only are the disabled covered, but caregivers of the disabled are also covered. The law protects both categories.

Q What is the key issue of the disability law?

A The central issue for an employer is the ability to perform the job functions. The law states that employers must "make reasonable accommodations" for the job for the person to perform the essential functions of that job. However, included in the assessment for disability are the set routines of daily living (McKee 1993, p. 19).

Q As the human resource director of a moderately small company in a community with a large community college rehabilitation program, we have decided to invest in several handicapped employees. My CEO and I have been pleased with the way this program has gone, until now. We cannot continue to cover the full benefits we offer to some of our full-time employees and also cover the extensive expenses of several of these employees. In fact, we may need to discontinue this joint work–study program, a move we hate to make. When I read the new laws I become confused about the rights or needs to cover disability benefits. Is it just me?

A Absolutely not. The laws are vague on this point; there is an apparent contradiction between an early section pertaining to discrimination of benefits for disabled, and the later section regarding insurance. The contradiction pertains to the statements in the law where Section 1630.4 describes prohibited discrimination, however, Section 36.212 allows insurance carriers to use disability factors in risk calculations (McKee 1993, p. 20). These are apparent contradictions within the disability law.

Q We have a commitment to hiring the physically challenged. Now we are considering excluding from their benefits package any preexisting problems. Can we do this?

A   It is highly possible with the new laws that such an exclusion would not be legal. Consult a legal advisor for further specific details of your situation.

Q   Can we exclude certain illnesses from our coverage in the benefits package?

A   As long as you do not address certain disabilities you might, but it is not absolutely clear you will. The laws are confusing and somewhat vague; the thrust of the intent is nondiscrimination against certain disabilities. If you continue to exclude on the basis of a treatment and not the illness, you may be in the clear. Make sure you apply changes to all employees.

Q   I am not sure about the term public access placed into a recent law. What is it and how does it affect companies?

A   The law on public access refers to the regulation which went into effect in January of 1992 regarding disabilities. Access must be provided to all employees in equal manner under this Americans with Disabilities Act. However, you are not the only employer who is unsure about the ramifications or the specifics of the law.

Q   How can I handle telling the disabled employees about pending cuts? It seems they have a different level of investment in health care and benefits.

A   While there are no data to substantiate your perception, you can imagine that a person with a disability requiring medical care would have a different level of investment in health care benefits. It would be helpful, prior to talking with this individual, if you knew how they used the present package for health care benefits. For example, are there medications covered now not covered in the future that this individual employee needs? How essential and how costly is this medication? Having this information can help you to respond in the appropriate sensitive manner you would want to do for any employee.

Q   Some of my employees are more concerned with dependents than with their own health care benefits. How do I resolve that?

A   You cannot be responsible for the value employees place on health care benefits, or the manner in which they arrive at that priority. However, if you do find a number of your employees are concerned with coverage for their dependents, consider it in the final decision regarding your company's package and the range of reductions or outright cuts in coverage.

Q   We plan to discontinue treatment coverage for certain blood donations. We want to make sure the change will not get us into trouble with the recent disabilities laws. What do you think?

A   If you exclude on a disability-specific basis, you may be in trouble. However, if you can apply the exclusion to all employees, you may be fine.

Q   We are not sure our current compensation package for workers fits with the new disability laws. How can we determine if the package and laws fit together?

A   Compare the criteria with your package to make sure that your benefits package and the laws fit with each other. Match and check policies of each to see whether they are in line with—complement—each other (McKee 1993, p. 20).

Q   How much information do human resource directors give employees?

A   All employees have a right to know their full benefits package and a right to written information in a clearly communicated manner. Also, employees, as well as administrators or managers, need to have enough advance warning of changes to make appropriate or alternative plans. With these general rules in mind, the human resource director can make a decision on how much information to convey and in what manner.

Q   What does it take to get all employees invested in benefits changes reflecting a proactive benefits program?

A   Change is always difficult, however, one needs to think of issues, such as the one reflected in this question, in order to plan strategies for constructive change. A first step is assessing the employee pool. Once this has been accomplished, the human resource director can determine in what manner to convey the information, and how much information to give at any one time.

Q   Our employees assume by cutting back we mean cutting out. Do you have examples of strategies where cutting back resulted in both quality and economical coverage?

A   Absolutely. Take Oxford, a managed-care service in southwest Connecticut (Touby 1993, p. 96). They recently reported a cutback option they are considering—to offer corporate clients who use doctors who are considered low cost a break in price of somewhere between 10 and 15 percent. Consider, also, that Oxford reports high quality, consumer satisfaction, and price reduction in benefits, all attractive features to corporate clients.

Q   Many small companies are concerned with the problems of raising deductibles. Is there a best way to approach this problem?

A No. There is no one right way to increase a deductible. However, the size of your company's projected increase may serve as a guide. If it is large, a major proportion of the total, allow more time. Or if increases also include major elimination or cuts also allow more time for adjustments. If the raise is a slight increase over in-place plans implement it as soon as appropriate notification can be given to employees.

Q We want to move away from offering any benefits to our employees' dependents. However, we are a company focused on high technology and most of our employees are relatively young with dependents at home. What can we do?

A One popular area to cut is the employee dependent. However, you will need to decide what to cut with a company assessment. If after making an assessment of your situation you still want to cut, plan accordingly. Allow enough time for your employees to find an adequate alternative plan. It would be prudent to offer some suggestions to employees, perhaps draw up a list of alternatives for them. Having some dollar figures on the cost saving will also help to ease the final decision for those affected employees.

Q A bright young employee with a number of dependents came into my office recently to discuss our proposed health care changes. He stated the quality of the services we offered would go down because we planned to shift from an individual physician service to another form of practice. He brought with him a sheaf of papers with statistics on the ratings of other types of groups. I got defensive rather than proactive. What should I have said?

A Getting an employee to buy into a new plan is at least a two-step process. First, you have to deal with the initiation of change; if the previous benefits offering is perceived as positive the task will be harder. Second, you need to initiate a change for something perceived as another valued good. With these steps in mind, get statistics to substantiate your change. You had rationale for making the change, so use those data to talk with your concerned employee. The bottom line is also relevant: Companies that lose do not retain employees for long.

FAMILY LEAVES

Q   We are considering providing family leave in our current benefits package. I say it is a good idea but my boss says it is too expensive. What should we do?

A   Check your sources, but you may not have a choice. According to the Family Leave Bill, signed February of 1993, which went into effect in August of 1993, workers have the right to family leave. Expense may not be the issue.

Q   My employees are asking for three months of paid leave under this new family leave program. We are thinking of offering six weeks. Will that be all right?

A   Probably not. The law specifies that a company must provide 12 weeks (Maynard 1993, p. 26). It also specifies unpaid leave.

Q   Does it matter whether we are a small company when it comes to the Family Leave Bill?

A   Yes. Only companies with more than 50 employees now need to comply with the new laws (Maynard 1993, p. 26).

Q We provided a paid family leave for an employee who never returned to work. I want to recover the health care premiums we paid. Can we do that?

A Absolutely. Although you are required to continue coverage, if an employee does not return to work your company is entitled to recover premiums it paid out (Maynard 1993, p. 26).

Q An employee dropped by to talk to me about the plans he and his wife are making. They are planning to adopt a one-year-old child and he wants to take a family leave. Since there are no medical conditions with an adoption, I think it is unnecessary. How does the Family Leave Bill address this?

A The Family Leave Bill covers an employee in circumstances of adoption as well as a natural birth or a foster child.

Q An employee recently came to see me about her mother. She wants a leave to be with her mother, with whom she lives, during surgery and the following recovery period. It seems excessive. Is it?

A While it may seem excessive to the company, it is now covered under the new Family Leave Bill. The care provided to a parent, as well as to a child or spouse, is to be covered (Maynard 1993, p. 26).

Q A brand new employee came in to see me about staying home with his wife during the birth of their first child. He is asking for a 14-week leave. What can we do?

A There are several conditions. The leave bill states 12 weeks as the maximum per each year; the leave is unpaid. However, there are some areas like the District of Columbia that offer slightly longer time frames. If your company is based there, best check with an attorney.

Q   What about the fact that he is a new employee? I think he should be employed for longer in order to get this leave.

A   You are right about the assumption. The employee must have worked for 12 months and worked 1,250 hours in order to qualify for family leave under the new bill.

Q   It is expensive to provide health care benefits and since the family leave is unpaid, I am planning to drop the health care for the time an employee is away. Is this feasible?

A   Not so. You could get the company in trouble since the law specifies unpaid leave with continuing preexisting health care coverage.

Q   An employee just came to see me about a leave to be with his pregnant wife. He wants time off without pay starting next week. I think the request is unfair as he could have let us know sooner. Do I have to grant the leave?

A   Examining the bill on family leave will help. It states that the employee must give the company at least 30 days notice in what are called foreseeable cases (Maynard 1993, p. 26). One would assume that in this situation the leave is foreseeable, unless an emergent situation has occurred.

Q   We are a company in the private sector, and are not sure where we stand in relation to the new family leave laws as part of our benefits package. How can I find out?

A   The following states have provisions for the private sector on family leave: California, Connecticut, Hawaii, Maine, Minnesota, New Jersey, Oregon, Rhode Island, Vermont,

Washington, and Wisconsin (Maynard 1993, p. 26). If your company is in one or more of these states, check for details.

Q   As the director of human resources, I feel like I am being taken advantage of with some new bills. I have several employees in good positions that I need to keep filled that are contemplating taking the maximum family leave. I don't want to get caught in a discrimination suit, but they could take these long leave periods. What, if anything, can I do?

A   You have several options even within the new Family Leave Bill. If your company grants the leaves and they are implemented, the company has the right to contact the employee while the worker is on leave to obtain information regarding his or her intentions for returning to work or not and their leave status (Maynard 1993, p. 26).

Q   Some of our highly compensated employees are discussing taking family leave. Is it true they may not be qualified to take the leave?

A   Yes. It will depend on where employees rank in terms of their compensation and how the company calculates it. A company may assess the top 10 percent of the employees and exempt them from the family leave coverage. Perhaps one or all of these employees fall into that category.

Q   A valued employee who has worked for us for a number of years, attaining promotions and increasing his position and rank in our company, is taking a family leave and wants to make sure the same job will be available to him. He came in last week with a magazine with the bill discussed. He claims the statement on equivalency means the same job is guaranteed. He said "equivalent" means "same." I don't think I can guarantee it but I am not sure what to do. What leeway do I have in this situation since we are currently downsizing our moderate sized company of 250 employees?

A It is accurate an employee or employees who take family leave cannot be discriminated against, or more to the point, penalized by having their jobs changed or reduced in position or wages when they return. The law specifically states that an equivalent job must be available to them. By definition the intent is an equal job with regard to salary and responsibilities and position. It does not, however, mean that the same job or position will be available.

Q I have an employee who wants to take a family leave. He only wants a few weeks to get his mother moved and established in a long-term nursing facility. Can he do that—use only a portion of his family leave?

A Absolutely. An employee may take up to a maximum of 12 weeks of unpaid family leave per year, but it does not specify that the entire amount must be used, nor does it mean that it must be taken all at once.

Q If an employee is only on family leave for a few weeks, it would seem a guarantee for the same job to be available would be possible. Does this seem realistic?

A While it may seem realistic, it would not be advisable to guarantee more than the law specifies. If you move to specify or guarantee the same job, you may end up in a difficult situation. There is too much that is unpredictable, including the amount of time the employee is actually on leave.

Q If an employee asks for less leave than the maximum, the 12 weeks, and decides she needs more, do we need to grant the extra amount?

A According to the law you would. However, no court cases are known at this time in which the issue has been pressed. The employee has a right to 12 weeks per year as the maximum amount. While employees, and employers, would ideally plan for the exact time needed and used, given the reasons employees take leaves it should also be anticipated alterations will be needed. When employees request less than the maximum amount, make plans allowing for extension contingencies.

Q After assessing an employment situation in which an employee requests a family leave, we find we need the employee. Since we are a smaller company, can we refuse to grant the leave?

A You might but check with an attorney. As noted above, the law states the 12 weeks. If for example, you and the employee agreed in writing to less time, and it is difficult to locate a replacement employee for the job, the company might have a burden claim. However, this is doubtful.

Q What can we do to prevent problem situations from happening in the future?

A Prior to implementation of a family leave sit down with the employee and go over the specifics. Discuss each criterion, especially job equivalency. Make sure the employee understands the features and the implications. Get a signed statement noting you have discussed each item with the employee. If, in addition, you anticipate a number of job changes in your company let the employee know and assure him or her that you will meet the specific requirements and do your best to offer the same position. However, if you cannot, you must provide him or her with an equivalent position.

Q A supervisor in our firm granted two family leaves in the same work area. Now the work area and the jobs are changing and I am afraid these two people will be angry. What can I do?

A As a courtesy and first step it would be wise to call and let the employees know there have been changes in their positions. Assure them the company will comply with the Family Leave Bill and that equivalent positions will be available for them when they return. Put all of this in writing, forwarding a letter to the employees. If they want to come in and discuss the situation, they should be encouraged to do so. A point to be made in these situations is the constantly changing work environment, as illustrated by their job situations. Keep good documentation, including job descriptions, qualifications, and total compensation package for each of the positions. Documentation will be used to verify job equivalency. If these are in place, and the jobs are equivalent, then the employees probably do not have a legitimate complaint, even though they may be angry.

Q We want to make sure we comply with this new Family Leave Bill. However, we are not sure what we need to keep in the way of documentation. What about records on family leaves as part of our benefits package?

A Records are essential to keep in this area as they are in all areas of benefits and coverage. Federal guidelines published in June 1993 established what is needed in recordkeeping (Maynard 1993, p. 26).

Q What company records should I keep to document our compliance with family leave?

A Although records are always important, it is suggested a minimum would be a signature from the employee, a description of his or her present job and the one to which the employee returns, dates and times, and length of leave (Maynard 1993, p. 26). In addition, I would suggest a "leave contract" including the intention of the employee to return to work. Document the details of the leave arrangement and any negotiations pertaining to it.

HIGH-RISK EMPLOYEES

Q If we want to limit coverage for a high-risk group of disability complaints, what should our focus be?

A Start with your own employees. However, the high-risk group usually includes those with back pain or disability emanating from back pain. Back pain and back-related injuries account for more than 15 percent of all complaints (McKee 1993, p. 22).

Q What is second highest among the frequent health complaints?

A The second highest is mental illness and related complaints, according to EEOC data (McKee 1993, p. 22). The proportion is around 8 percent.

Q What can be done with costly employees in terms of benefits?

A This is difficult because you cannot treat employees individually within the framework of a health care benefits package, as noted earlier regarding the individual employee who has a disability. However, in planning for reductions you will need to assess the costly employee along with the total claims package of a particular year. These data will give you information about how to plan reductions. In terms of an individual employee, if you only have one or two such individuals and are already aware of their concerns it would be gracious to have a conversation about the implications the proposed reductions have for them. While you cannot change the final decision, letting an employee know that you are aware of the situation, you are sensitive to the implications for them, and that you will try to do what you can certainly conveys a more concerned and positive message than simply forwarding all individuals the written material on the final decision.

Q We want to find out more about specifics regarding disabilities to protect our company in the future. Is there a place to turn to get information on disabilities?

A Yes. The federal government has established a national toll-free number to offer assistance: 1-800-949-4232. In addition, there are now ten facilities called Disability & Technical Assistance Centers, which may be more locally accessible to you.

Q Is it true that a company pool of high-risk employees would help to save us money?

A Maybe. However, if you place all your high-risk employees into one company pool, you lose the option of spreading their risks over the larger pool of your total employees (Maynard 1993, p. 26). While a pool such as you suggest might get some of the higher-risk employees a less expensive form of benefits for the company to purchase, in the long run it might be more expensive for the larger numbers of employees than if you did not use a pool. Company size is a factor in this situation.

Q Our high-risk employees are discussing the possibility of cosharing more of their health care coverage. However, overall they are displeased. It there a way of making it more palatable?

A Yes. Discuss it in light of the total impact on the company. Data are always helpful.

Q There is such a trend today toward managed health care, but we think our physically challenged and high-risk employees are not aware of this. Do other employees resist these changes?

A Of course. Money is involved, and in some cases substantial amounts, as you well know. Do not get into underlying motivations. Try these strategies: Provide the employees with clear information and statistical data on your company; describe what others in similar situations are doing; what companies of the same size are doing; and the overall effect on the firm. These usually offer enough information to serve as an incentive.

JOB STRESS

Q An employee came to talk with me and started to tell me about her job. She eventually told me that she was having difficulty in her work. She complained about headaches, about tension at work, and in sum, described stress. What do others do about stress or burnout on the job? How does one know if it is, indeed, legitimate stress or burnout?

A Fortunately, diagnosis is not your job. Refer her to a specialist who can assess her problems. However, you have tapped into one area raising suspicions the most frequently among claims employees present (McKee 1993, p. 22).

Q Last week, four of our employees discussed claims for stress on the job. They cited everything from postal workers and stress to turnover in other fields. How prevalent is job stress?

A   According to a Northwestern National Life Insurance study conducted in 1991, among American workers one in three gave consideration to leaving their jobs and cited stress as the contributing factor (McKee 1993, p. 23).

Q   Of all the areas I dread the most as the director of human resources and benefits, I dread a lawsuit and a claim for disability related to job stress. What can I do to protect myself in this situation?

A   Document, document, document! Keep accurate records and get an employee signature when you discuss items, issues, or portions of the situation so they, too, can become a part of the recordkeeping. Good records and documentation are the keys to prevention in situations you describe. Stress as a job disability is a claim that generates enormous discussion among benefits administrators and claims lawyers (McKee 1993, p. 23).

Q   Some of our high-risk employees think we are hiding information from them. They claim we make a lot of money, and that our CEO is getting a large salary. They are really getting assertive about the company's new insistence on cosharing of benefits and changes in health care coverage. Any suggestions?

A   Take a hard look at the charges. If they are accurate and the information is public you may have a difficult situation on your hands to persuade the employees these changes are needed. If, however, they are not that accurate, provide correct information. In addition, some companies are using either a joint employee and manager board or an advisory board. The board meets to discuss the changes on a regular basis with representation from throughout the company, including high-level management. These discussions can go a long way in smoothing relations between labor and management.

Q How does one go about developing a board?

A You can use a number of strategies. The employees could elect representatives, or if you have a union it might be the union delegate, or you might have a joint election and appointment. Assess the strategy in light of the environment. If there is a high level of trust then either will work; if not, you need to use more time in assessing and implementing a joint strategy.

Q We have recently decided to drop the dependent coverage as part of our package for our employees. However, several employees now tell me their families will go uncovered. Is there a viable solution?

A Several ideas come to mind. First, see if there are options among, for instance, working spouses. Second, you might offer the option of the employee continuing to purchase dependent coverage by paying directly. Last, if the latter is not a viable option, perhaps a compromise is: Allow them to continue paying directly for a limited time period, such as six months or a year, after which the coverage can be dropped.

REFERENCES

Maynard, R. 1993. Meet the new law on family leave. *Nation's Business*, April: 26.

McKee, B. 1993. The disabilities labyrinth. *Nation's Business*, April: 18–26.

Touby, L. 1993. Who's afraid of health reform? *Business Week*, 31 May: 96–97.

5

Managed-Care and Health Care Benefits

This chapter introduces the concept of managed care and discusses it in terms of similar concepts such as managed competition. The director of human resources is given clues to assess managed care as a possible option for his or her company. While managed care is looming on the horizon, there are a number of approaches to it. This chapter provides an overview of the critical issues and problems, defines terms, and suggests strategies for their resolution.

MANAGED CARE: STRATEGY FOR COST CONTAINMENT

Q   What exactly is managed care?

A   *Managed care* refers to the provision of total service by one provider who manages the care for consumers.

Q   Where did managed care start and was it successful in that setting?

A   One of the first reports was from New England Medical Center in the Northeast, back in the 1980s. It was, and is, successful.

Q   Is the organization continuing to use managed care?

A   Yes. When a company starts and then disbands an idea or model it is telling. However, most companies that initiated managed care are continuing to use it. More and more companies are coming on board with variations among their managed-care models.

Q   Is it true managed care as a model can be applied to a variety of services?

A   Yes. Management of care as a model for health care delivery can be overlaid on a number of prior models. And we will undoubtedly see more applications in the not-too-distant future.

Q   What kind of rating does managed care receive?

A   It depends on what you read but there are strong indicators that it is highly rated. For example, a survey of consumers in one HMO, a form of managed care, compared satisfaction with HMOs to national reports on consumer satisfaction with care. In the survey, consumer satisfaction was 94 percent compared to the national average of satisfaction of 79 percent (McNamee et al. 1993, p. 121).

Q   How will managed care decrease our benefits costs?

A   Managed care decreases overall costs by providing reimbursement for a norm or average range of services for certain illnesses or treatments, such as surgery. As these costs for illness or treatment are recognized by the reimbursement agency you use, the decreases should pass on to you. Also, if you do not offer certain benefits, the company will decrease its overall payout.

Q   What are critical paths?

A   In the new environment for health care reform, a *critical path* is essentially an anticipated or expected route a particular patient-consumer would follow for a diagnosis, treatment, or hospitalization. It is the minimum essential anticipated path for a consumer's care per diagnosis or illness.

Q   What is a path variance?

A   The *variance* is the opposite of the critical path; it is the difference in the amount of time and treatment used. Variance is unanticipated. The variance is essentially the patient care needed which is not on the path or is unanticipated in the critical path. For example, a patient admitted for bypass surgery may develop a blood clot creating the need for longer than anticipated hospitalization. The difference between the anticipated and unanticipated is the variance.

Q   What do variances have to do with our company?

A   Variance translates into dollars and increased costs in claims, depending on the rationale for the variance and the perceived or projected cause. Concepts of critical path and variance directly affect your company if paths are developed which are quite tight, if they are implemented stringently, and if the company has a number of individuals for whom the paths are not appropriate or for whom there is frequent variance.

Q   What are some suggestions for prevention of problems when we get into managed care?

A   The major change is the difference between what was reimbursed in the past, and what is covered in today's climate either in terms of benefits or in terms of what is offered in local facilities. The idea of having a professional discuss the difference is a good way to avoid employee complaints. For example, if an employee knows that in the past all medications were fully covered, and tomorrow only 50 percent will be, employees need to rethink the medications they request and are using. Also, a candid conversation about the positive use and savings of generic medications, for example, is a preventive measure.

Q   There must be some way to assess the quality of managed care. What is it?

A   Data on managed care are beginning to pour in. While there are always differences there are some key criteria. Inquire about the physicians on the payroll: Are they board-certified and in what specialty? Where were they educated and where was their specialized training? Was it a quality site? A national standard suggested as a criterion or target for the percentage of HMO physicians who are board-certified in their specialty is about 70 percent (Doctor network 1993, p. 113). In addition, get information on the form doctors fill out to join the practice, which the organization should be willing to give to you. See if verification of education and licensure is used on applications of physicians.

Q   Are there other positive examples of managed care with data to substantiate their claims?

A   An excellent example is a company in Connecticut called Oxford. It reported 91 percent board-certified physicians, a surge in revenue, and high quality control and consumer satisfaction (Touby 1993, p. 96). This is difficult to top, especially when they report premiums 30 percent lower than traditional insurance.

Q How will I, as the human resource director, know what illnesses or treatments come under managed care?

A Any illness or treatment can be placed under a managed-care model. In fact, hospitals and health clinics are currently developing what are called *care maps* or plans for patients and clients to route through their facilities.

Q Is it true some major carriers are shifting to a managed-care approach even though reform is not certain?

A Yes. A prominent example is the Empire Blue Cross and Blue Shield in New York State, which announced in the summer of 1993 it was moving toward a managed-care model (Frisch 1993, p. A16).

Q Is Empire going on managed care entirely? What are the implications if they do not?

A Empire announced it would begin to tailor restrictions for its "oldest and sickest customers" (Frisch 1993, p. A16). These customers are in their high-risk category as consumers of health care. If Empire is taking this position with high-risk customers, it implies they will implement other limits or extend their category.

Q What other implications does it have?

A One clear implication is high-risk categories or groups or customers, whether employees or not, will not be balanced by those in a low-risk category (Frisch 1993, p. A16). Empire noted in its announcement that this form of high risk–low risk subsidy was not working due to accelerating health care costs. Poor results do not bode well for the high-risk and costly employee.

Q   How much of a cost saving can my company anticipate with the introduction of managed care?

A   That will depend on the amount of outlay you had before and the amount of usage under the managed-care model. However, in general, it is anticipated providers would see about a 20 percent cut in costs for outlay of treatments. These reductions will vary, but the above percentage is an overall average. Remember these reductions are for use; not included are reductions for those benefits cut.

Q   How can I get my employees to think in terms of managed-care service?

A   Do you have a company nurse or physician? If not, then ask a health services administrator or a professional nurse who works in a managed-care facility to meet with employees. Ask providers to discuss managed care with employees.

Q   What if the above does not work?

A   It will take a while, but it should work if the employees intend to use the services you provide. In addition to information, tracing a common illness example followed through a care map or care route should be helpful. Give your employees a clear example of what the average or managed-care map will be for certain common illnesses or treatments. Select some for discussion that you see relatively often in your company claims. Back pain would be a good example. This way, workers begin to see what to anticipate and what not to anticipate.

Q   I am confused between the terms managed care and case management. What is the difference?

A   You are not alone. *Managed care* refers to a clinical system for the strategic management of cost and quality outcomes (McDaniel 1993, p. 51). Managed care is a competitive way to view health care whereas *case management* refers to a delivery of service whereby one provider, usually a nurse, will organize and coordinate services. The care provider will manage the total care of the patient: from admission through and until discharge including also the discharge planning.

HEALTH MAINTENANCE ORGANIZATIONS

Q   With all this talk about a health maintenance organization or HMO, I am not really sure I understand what it is. What is an HMO?

A   This is a very timely question. Essentially, an HMO is a comprehensive health care service providing 24-hour coverage using a prepaid plan for a comprehensive range of services (Mayer 1984). While the service may be comprehensive, there are some differences in the range and breadth of services offered. These should be checked, or compared, prior to signing on.

Q   When one compares an HMO with the type of service most of us know, the fee-for-service most physicians use, what are the key differences?

A   There are three key differences to address in comparing the HMO for your employees (Mayer 1984). They include an emphasis on the prevention of illness rather than payment for services for a treatment or illness, you pay not for each specific service but a flat monthly fee for all services, and all your health care will be delivered by that HMO. There may be case-by-case exceptions to these, but these three are the predominate differences between the traditional fee-for-service types of care and the newer HMO types of care.

Q   Aren't HMOs new and untried on the market?

A   No. In fact, the first HMO was in effect in 1929 but they did not really emerge in large numbers until the 1970s (Mayer 1984). Although they are not new, their rapid growth and the attention paid to them is relatively new.

Q   Just how fast is the HMO phenomenon growing?

A   In 1973, for example, there were 72 HMOs in the U.S., but a decade later there were 290 covering 42 states (Mayer 1984).

Q   Isn't the quality of care in most HMOs poor compared to other models?

A   Not necessarily. In surveys the quality of an HMO was rated at 77.3 percent satisfaction by consumers, whereas general offerings were rated by their consumers or patients at 65 percent (McNamee et al. 1984, p. 121).

Q   As we begin to assess changes, we want to explore health maintenance organizations. What are the key questions we should ask to decide if we should shift to an HMO?

A   There are a number but several sources suggest the following (Mayer 1984). In addition to costs of the monthly premiums, explore the overall track record of the HMO; its consumer satisfaction rating; benefit conversion for your employees; the number, range, and depth of the services; the supplemental sources; the quality of the providers, especially the ratings of physicians in the plan; the time spent waiting, as time can be an expensive employer outlay; any education for health provided; and the amount of control your company or an individual employee may have with HMOs. Even in an HMO there is need for some degree of control on the part of the consumer which includes both your firm and your employees.

Q Is there a report on the performance measures for HMOs?

A Yes. Sixty performance measures were assessed in a report by the National Committee for Quality Assurance (NCQA) to assist purchasers in obtaining HMO services (Mayer 1984).

Q What is the purpose of the NCQA information?

A This report provides a database through which a company can assess the facility as well as one for comparison of the various facilities in operation.

Q Why is this important and what implications will it have for our company?

A At the current time there is a great deal of variation in the way facilities report their outcomes as well as the ways in which they measure them (Mayer 1984). Obtaining similar measures will render comparable data for ease of comparison for buyers.

Q I understand in some HMOs there is a patient advocate which would seem to be an advantage for our employees. Is that true?

A Yes. Many HMOs do have patient advocates. One of the most successful is the Yale Health Plan in New Haven, CT, which has had a patient advocate for a number of years.

Q   Are there advantages to having a patient advocate?

A   The Yale plan has worked quite successfully. The role of a patient advocate is to enhance patient or consumer satisfaction and to reduce the overall costs for such expensive items as litigation. In terms of employees, for example, an HMO with a patient advocate would be quite advantageous. The advocate role is a complement to the benefits administrator role. In terms of enhancing patient/consumer satisfaction, prevention of litigation, and diffusing conflicts, the advocate role probably pays for itself three times over.

Q   Is a health maintenance organization the way to go?

A   It depends greatly on your package. If your company offers a full range of benefits obtained in an HMO, the form of service is, indeed, less costly in the long run. Most companies seem to think an HMO is a less costly service since the physicians are salaried and may offer a full complement of services for a company's employees.

Q   We are concerned that the HMO our company is planning to use may backfire on us. It is requesting a per employee premium of $5,000 per family. We think it is high, but, is it?

A   It is high, however, the amounts vary depending on the region, the number of employees, their risk factors, and what is actually covered in the program. Given these variations, you need to get national averages and compare what you are getting for those services and what is not covered.

Q   When we changed to an HMO, we were told the customer, our employees, had a choice of physicians, which was important to our workers. Now we are getting a lot of complaints that they do not have a choice when they go. What can I do?

A   Keep complete records of each worker's complaint, including the dates, times, and causes for service. Call and make an appointment to discuss the situation with the appropriate representative.

Q   My employees complain a lot about the new HMO we are using. The key issue is the choice they have in the selection of physicians. Just how much choice is available?

A   A great deal depends on employees' perceptions of choice, as well as their expectation. If they assumed they could retain their prior physician, they will undoubtedly feel less satisfied. However, if they were told initial choice was possible among several physicians at the HMO it is an appropriate message.

Q   We recently changed from a small to a larger HMO thinking our employees would be pleased. We gave them one month's notice. Now they are angry. What happened?

A   One month is not enough time to change appointments in most medical systems. A three-month notification period would be more realistic, especially if the service is large and relatively busy, as most are.

Q   Four of my employees told me that the new HMO we are using treats them like numbers. In fact, they say that whenever they call, the HMO does not ask for their name, just their number. Is this the way all HMOs operate?

A   Check your sources and check the information—call the HMO yourself, for example. It is true that most services need some means by which to identify the client or patient for identification and tracking purposes. After all, your workers do not want to get their records and thus their medications or treatments confused with those of other employees.

Q   Several of our older employees recently attended an open meeting we held to discuss health care benefits. They were angry that we were moving toward "socialized medicine" and they threatened a lawsuit against us. Do other directors have similar experiences?

A   Just about every situation has been reported somewhere. The issue, however, is how to address this situation within your own setting. Get more information on the HMO; sit down in another open meeting and have a discussion. Perhaps as a final step make an actual visit to the facility or have a representative visit your company; make sure those employees are present.

Q   Several of our employees who live near a large teaching hospital have family members not covered on their plan because of the additional cost. They use the local emergency room as their primary service; an HMO means a longer distance for them to travel. Do companies offer transportation to their facilities?

A   It would seem impossible to allow for the various residences of a company's employees and their families. An exception might be in a smaller town. However, if employees and their families could get to your company, it would be a bonus to have a van providing a round-trip to the HMO. You need to assess the cost and the benefits of this added service.

Q   We think perhaps providing transportation to an HMO might help employees to take advantage of the preventive aspect. Do any other companies do this?

A   Not that have been reported. However, you might consider a monthly van service for the annual exams and checkups that families need if you have enough employees to offer the service. Consider signing up employees and their families to maximize efficiency.

Q An employee tells me that the physician she used to have is now with an HMO. She wants to know if the doctor will continue to see her. What do most do?

A As providers go through a transition in care delivery, there will be more and more situations using a combination of payment types. Most physicians who had private patients and changed or also became affiliated with an HMO continue to see the private patients, at least their original ones. The employee should inquire; maybe the physician will only continue with former patients, and not take on new ones as a containment on the number of patients.

Q We are affiliated with an HMO which is also a part of a large university teaching hospital. When our employees are in the hospital they are besieged by a number of medical students. How can we get it stopped?

A It is not clear you can. Or, if you do it may increase your service fees. Residents, for example, make far less than a private physician of comparable training and are therefore much less costly. Inquire before you change.

Q Are there advantages to a group practice as a provider service over those of a health maintenance organization?

A There is usually an advantage perceived from the employees' perspective. There is a greater choice of physician; more provider choice on the part of the consumer which, in this situation, is your company's employee. In contrast, a group practice may not have the resources in personnel to offer as full a complement of services, ranging, for example, from obstetrics to surgery to internal medicine, as a health maintenance organization would. Again, it does depend on how one defines the group practice and what is included in the offering.

Q Is there a list of the best plans in the country and, if so, where can I get it?

A Several recent surveys are being published, with more coming out each week. For example, a recent survey by HealthPlus Management Services, published in *Money* magazine, evaluated 413 of the nation's 546 HMOs on 29 separate cost and quality measures (*Money* 1993, p. 111). The top three of the top ten were Kaiser's Foundation Health Plans in San Francisco and Los Angeles, and the Harvard Community Plan in Boston.

Q We have several employees who travel a lot. In fact, they are probably away more than they are in the office but it is an important part of their jobs. If we cut back and begin to use a health maintenance organization for our health care, will they be covered when they are traveling?

A It depends. They will be covered, but the trick is whether they can get service. Unless you have a mutual agreement with an HMO in the area where they have a need for service, and if HMOs are willing to provide treatment/service, your employees will be without coverage. In addition, the HMO may be of different quality or may not offer the specific services needed. This is probably the key disadvantage of an HMO.

Q We have several companies in California. California seems to have a lot of health maintenance organizations. Is this information accurate, because, if it is we may want to change our employees over to an HMO in that state?

A   Of all the states, California has the largest participation with more than 30.6 percent of its population HMO enrolled in 1991 (Piacentini and Foley 1992).

Q   What about other states? Do all states have health maintenance services?

A   No, but that will undoubtedly change. For example, in 1991 only Wyoming, Mississippi, and Alaska did not have HMOs (Piacentini and Foley 1992).

Q   How prevalent are health maintenance organizations in the U.S.? We need to locate several.

A   You would probably be able to locate one in most areas since there are over 556 typical HMOs in the U.S. as of the early part of the decade (Piacentini and Foley 1992); the number is increasing.

Q   What is the range of population proportions enrolled in HMOs in the U.S.?

A   Of those states with an HMO, the low is 0.8 percent in Montana, to 30.6 percent in California; the next is Minnesota with 25.6 percent (Piacentini and Foley 1992).

Q   Is it true the proportion of the U.S. population enrolled in HMOs is low?

A   At the early part of the 1990s more than 14 percent were enrolled; it is growing (Piacentini and Foley 1992).

PHYSICIAN PROVIDER ORGANIZATIONS

Q   I understand that the physician provider groups or organizations (PPOs) are not cost-effective. Am I right?

A   Surveys vary in their results, however, there are some early indicators they may not be as cost-effective as one would like. For example, a study conducted at the University of Michigan found some PPOs were costing more than traditional insurance (McNamee et al. 1993, p. 115). The Michigan study compared 14 similar plans and had some physician choice among the PPOs.

Q   A number of people in benefits administration are exploring the option of a physician grouping. They suggest physician costs in fee-for-service are high. Is this true?

A   It seems to be. Recent surveys report that among the nation's 615,000 physicians, about 75 to 80 percent of the costs of the health care system were driven by them (Flynn 1993, p. 95). This explains some physician resistance to reform, since one implication for doctors is less reliance on fee-for-service practices.

Q   Preferred provider organizations seem to be a transitional form of service. What does that mean?

A   PPOs have been found costly in some studies. They have also been suggested as a transition toward a managed-care type of delivery service, and as a means to shift employees away from fee-for-service delivery of care (McNamee et al. 1993, p. 115). PPOs, however, may not survive as a viable form of health care delivery.

Q   There are so many descriptions of physician group practices (PGPs). What is a PGP?

A   A *physician group practice* is a network of physicians who form a collective and arrange payments to the collective. They will usually offer tests and procedures previously offered in hospitals (Cerne 1993, p. 28). What may differ is the means they use to distribute funds coming into the group. For example, in some instances with a senior and junior partner, physicians divide all revenues on a proportionate basis. In others, the physicians may divide on the basis of number of clients seen. In any event, the group offers services and coverage via a group of physicians.

Q   Several of my employees are asking about the possibility of joining some physician group practices. A budget analyst in our company is especially adamant that these are questionable. What are the data on this form of service?

A   As an increasingly important part of the total picture of the health care delivery system, physician group practices are more popular. Recent ratings suggest that several are outstanding. The factors in these ratings include such items as the history, implementation, revenue growth, and competition. Overall, they are rated relatively high (Cerne 1993, p. 28).

Q   If we no longer use "fee-for-service" providers, how will it affect us?

A   Depending on your benefits package it may be a minimum difference. For example, if you did not provide full coverage for some fee-for-service providers, then a change will not be dramatic. If you did have full coverage, moving to a health maintenance organization, to cite one example, means you would be paying less for service than the company did in the past. Your company would see a cost saving.

DIAGNOSTIC RELATED GROUPS

Q   What are DRGs?

A   A *diagnostic related group* (DRG) is a concept introduced in 1982 in order to allow groups or categories of illnesses and, therefore, their treatment to be addressed as a norm. It was essentially a means of standardizing or determining a norm for certain categories of care. In today's medical jargon there are over 450 DRGs which are used in admitting and providing diagnostic treatment categories for patients.

Q   Do all patients fall under DRGs?

A   While most diagnoses do there are services that do not. For example, most surgical procedures do, while no psychiatric hospitalizations do currently, although it is predicted they will in the near future.

Q   What implications do DRGs have for our cuts?

A   The actual implications are not clear at this time. If the number and range of DRGs expand, then psychiatric services might fall under covered hospitalizations. A company may want to reexamine its benefits, or lack of benefit, regarding psychiatric hospitalization, for example.

Q   How will preadmission certification affect our health care benefits package?

A   Certification is a control and cost containment measure on the part of insurers. Prior to forwarding payment for a claim, the insurer will obtain certification that the treatment—especially surgery—is necessary. Once certified, the claim will be paid. However, if the claim is not certified or denied, then, if the employee receives the service, he or she may pay out-of-pocket for that health service.

MOVING TOWARD HEALTH

Q   I want to motivate my employees toward better health. What kinds of programs can I plan to accomplish this goal?

A   Begin by planning programs that emphasize good health and a healthy attitude. Reward health, not illness; prevention, rather than cure. Place the emphasis on the preventive measures known to reduce health risks. Smoking cessation is one of these, as is weight loss. Exercise and healthy diet are others. In addition, plan a program providing examination for potential illnesses, such as mammographies or annual checkups, rather than rewarding illness and hospitalization.

Q   Will a change in our deductible adversely affect our use of physicians?

A   That will depend, of course, on the reimbursements that your physicians now use. In addition, it will also depend on the range of services as well as the degree of physician choice you intend to continue for your employees. However, if your employees currently have relatively free choice in their use of physicians, a raise in deductible may decrease the range of physician use. Again, it will depend on the arrangement with physicians between you and your company as well as the type of benefit you offer to your employees.

Q   One of our more senior employees came in to see me yesterday. She has been seeing the same physician for decades, and she wants to continue. Her question was, "Will I be able to continue seeing my doctor?" What should I tell her?

A   Depending on the changes you make in your benefits, it is very likely an employee may continue with the same physician. However, your response depends on your company changes. An honest response is to tell her you will certainly try to have employees continue with their regular physicians and it is to everyone's advantage, including yours and hers, to have continuity in care. Until you know for sure what changes will be put into place a guarded response is in order.

Q   Several of our employees like to meet for coffee and a smoke outside the plant for their daily break. When they meet, their primary conversation is about their latest illness or most recent surgery. How can I get them to think in terms of health and prevention rather than illness and treatment?

A   You need to rethink the meaning of social circles and informal systems in an organization. These may serve as important vehicles for company performance. One solution is to offer a healthy substitute for smoking but one that involves some informal group relationships and communication; breaks with healthy snacks or a walk around your facility, for example. On the other hand, you might introduce the concept of health by indicating your company is less interested in illness than health and offer specific instances like those noted above. Reward healthy behavior.

COMMUNICATING THE MESSAGE

Q   What are some strategies for communicating the message my company wants to get across?

A   You have made the first step which is to determine you have a message and need to communicate it. After deciding what you want to communicate, use several means to convey it—company meetings, the inside newspaper or newsletter, bulletin boards, and informal conversations. Ask your midlevel managers to get the message to their subordinates. When you meet with employees, let them know you have a new message. The communication channels you used in the past, given they were successful and the message was clear, should work for this one.

Q   We want to convey health and prevention. How do we do that?

A   The most obvious and direct way is to tell company employees. Rewards you set up for employees will convey and reinforce the primary message. The primary message can be enforced with such examples as a health club, a walking group, or arrangements for employees to use a local gym during lunch. Use the employee cafeteria to illustrate your message and follow up with an explicit message. Offer healthy alternative meals and list the nutritional content. Last, get the CEO to eat a healthy meal and jog with employees!

Q   My employees are trying to understand the changes in benefits. One suggestion they share with each other is to shop around. Is this a viable alternative and what are the implications for us as a company?

A   Get your employees to work for you, by all means! If they find a more cost-efficient system, find out what it is. Use their feedback. The process of shopping around, which is distressing to some providers, is also the way to keep costs down.

Q   We are thinking of forming an employee discussion group. What should the focus be?

A   Use this group to get feedback and help your employees understand the changes. Find out what they like and have them discuss it with coworkers. If any of them have positive data, use these to start the discussion. Avoid a negative outcome by focusing the discussion or by providing structure for the discussion.

REFERENCES

Cerne, F. 1993. Balancing complex choices. *Hospitals & Health Networks*, 20 June: 28–30.

Doctor network. 1993. *Money*, July: 111–13.

Flynn, J. 1993. The final option: Radical surgery. *Business Week*, 11 January: 95.

Fritsch, J. 1993. Empire moving toward managed care. *New York Times*, 20 July: A16.

Mayer, T., & Mayer, G. 1984. *The Health Insurance Alternative: A Complete Guide to Health Maintenance Organizations.* New York: Perigee Books.

McDaniel, C. 1993. Organizational systems that support management of care. *Managing Nursing Care, Series in Nursing Administration*, vol. 3, ed. K. Kelly.

McNamee, M., Weber, J., & Mitchell, R. 1993. Health care reform: It's already here. *Business Week*, 11 January: 95.

Piacentini, J., and Foley, J. 1992. *EBRI Databook on Employee Benefits, 2nd ed.* Washington, D.C.: Employee Benefits Research Institute.

Touby, L. 1993. Who's afraid of health reform? *Business Week*, 31 May: 96–97.

6

Flexible Benefits and Employee Options

One of the most challenging decisions regarding benefits and their changes is the issue of flexibility or options for employees. While options are always attractive, there are limits on what and how many can be offered. This chapter explores a variety of problems emerging for companies that desire some flexibility and employee options, yet want to conserve their company resources. As a guide for the director of human resources key issues concerning flexible benefits and employee options are explored with suggestions.

FLEXIBLE PLANS FOR HEALTH BENEFITS

Q   When did flexible benefits plans start?

A   The plan has been around a long time, if one considers the modest choices allowed employees in the past, such as whether to purchase or to extend life insurance or to cover dependents. However, the form most companies use when referring to a flex plan became more popular in the 1970s and expanded in the 80's (Foster 1986).

Q   Isn't a flexible plan the same thing as a menu or cafeteria plan?

A   A *flexible* benefit is another term for what is known as the cafeteria plan, as well as a variable benefit, or a flexible compensation package. A menu plan is not the same.

Q   Our CEO is interested in having our office explore a flex plan. What is a flex plan?

A   To some degree this depends on the term. In most cases *flex plans* or flexible benefits plans for health care coverage offer a range of choices from which an employee may select.

Q   Was there a company that introduced the flex plan?

A   Yes. It started in 1974 with the TRW Defense and Space Systems Group, Inc., based in California.

Q   What were the core points of the TRW plan?

A   Health care and life insurance.

Q   Was it a true flexible benefits plan?

A   No. Ironically, the original plan was called a hybrid among flex plans. It offered a midrange between the more traditional nonflex plans and the wholly flexible plans of today. It used only two options (Foster 1986).

Q   Is the story of the TRW company a true success story? I thought they stopped the plan.

A   Not so. TRW, which started with a few employees on the plan, covers over 11,000 employees and continues to use the flexible benefits plan (Foster 1986).

Q   How many employees are covered under flexible plans today?

A   Figures from the late 1980s show that among the full-time work force in firms with more than 100 employees, a little over 24 percent are covered by a flexible benefits plan (Foster 1986). These data did not specify which type of flex plan.

Q   Isn't it true there are few employees participating in flexible benefits plans and reimbursement accounts?

A   Among full-time employees in private medium and large firms, only 9 percent participated in 1989 (Piacentini and Foley 1992).

Q   We are a government agency and some of my employees want to get into a more flexible benefits arrangement. However, the government has not used flexible plans to any great degree, or has it?

A   Among full-time employees in the local and state agencies, only 5 percent participated in flexible plans in large and medium agencies.

Q   Since we are a small private firm, we assume we would not be able to offer a flexible plan. Is this true of most companies our size?

A   Probably. Only 1 percent of employees in private and small companies participated in a flexible benefits plan at the turn of the decade.

Q Why is growth so slow among the companies that are offering flexible plans? We want to start one but want to avoid problems.

A It seems to be a matter of size and resources; the two are related. The larger the firm, the more resources, and thus ability to provide a truly flexible benefits plan.

Q What is the main reason for the success of the flexible plan?

A The increase in numbers of workers who want a flexible plan is a response to the changing needs of the American family and the work force. Flex plans cater to the diverse needs of families represented by our employees and their demands.

Q Are there certain categories of workers who seem to participate more in flexible plans than others?

A Yes. Statistics reflect a larger proportion of professional and administrative participants, with 14 percent participation, and technical and clerical, with 15 percent participation (Piacentini and Foley 1992).

Q What category has the lowest participation among workers?

A Production and service workers have little representation among flexible plans—3 percent (Piacentini and Foley 1992).

Q Is this a reflection of participation or of the availability of the flexible plan option?

A Data only reflect the level of participation but does not include the motivation behind participation (Piacentini and

Foley 1992). One would not know from the data whether the flexible plan was an employee option or not.

Q What other companies have had success with the flexible plan? We want to compare our relatively professionally oriented company to others of similar size.

A A similar company might be the Educational Testing Service in New Jersey, which offers a wide range of choices to its employees, many of whom are in professional categories (Foster 1986). Other examples are Thomas Jefferson University in Philadelphia and the American Can Company based in Greenwich, CT.

Q I hear companies are doing away with their flex plans. Is this true?

A Not so. There is a gradual increase in the numbers of workers both seeking and being covered by a flexible benefits plan.

Q Is it true the IRS does not recognize flex plans?

A No. Section 125 of the Internal Revenue Code acknowledged flexible benefits in 1978 (Foster 1986).

Q We want to be more flexible. Where do we start?

A Start by assessing where your company is now. Get a clear picture of your company possibilities, obtain from your boss the amount of outlay desired for benefits and, in particular, the health care benefits factor. Match this information with data on prior claims and employee desires.

Q What is the basic principle of flexible plans?

A The essence of a flexible benefits plan is to allow a close tailoring or match between the needs of the employees and the plan offered (Foster 1986). This implies a good knowledge of one's employees.

Q   Just how much "flex" do we need to make our plan flexible?

A   Flexibility will depend on two things. One is the range of choice your employees want and will exercise. The second is the degree of range of choice that your company can afford to offer. Although a standard format is often implied, there is no standard format for a flex plan. You may offer a list of choices that fit your employees' needs and your company's possibilities; you may also attempt to encourage prevention or health with certain choices in a flex plan. Likewise, you may want to encourage some options that employees may not typically use, or of which they may not be aware; put them on the menu list.

Q   Don't most companies have a few items that are always covered, even if they have a flex plan?

A   Yes. Most employees have a core of items offered by most companies. Employee hospitalization is a good example of a core item.

Q   What if we want to cover something our employees do not want?

A   Assess the impact on your company both in terms of the cost and the risk. A good example of an item you would probably want to offer and the employees may not value as highly as you do, is disability coverage.

Q   We are concerned the management of a flexible benefits plan may be more than we can handle. Do others find this to be true?

A   Yes and no. If you keep the choices relatively limited and the differences clear, it will be more manageable. The management issues arise with numerous changes or when employees do not understand the choices and distinctions (Foster, 1986).

Q   We think the administration of a flexible benefits plan is a problem. My boss wants us to explore it. What do other administrators say?

A   Experts acknowledge the initiation of a flexible benefits plan is not for the inept (Foster 1986). It takes experience and time to set up and to administer well. It is a challenging task.

Q   What are the problems of the long-term maintenance of a flexible benefits plan?

A   Once in place it is no more difficult to administer than any other plan. The challenge is in setting it up.

Q   Do flexible benefits plans save their companies money?

A   It is a vital consideration in today's market. Unfortunately, the flexible benefits plans do not save any more money than other types (Foster 1986), especially compared to the managed-care models. However, cost containment is not the main aim of the flexible benefits plans.

Q   What data are there about how employees handle the flexible benefits plans? We have a small company with a number of relatively young employees. Will they do well?

A   There are always going to be employees who do not select well and others who do. A young and relatively inexperienced work group may have less need for a wide range of options and may need more assistance. There may be other rationales, however, for offering it. Overall, reports note employees have made good choices.

Q   I hear flexible plans may soon be obsolete. Is this true?

A   Not entirely, although there are warnings that reforms projected into the twenty-first century may change them. Surveys suggest some reform ideas may eliminate flex plans due to the loss of federal tax subsidy that is an advantage of flexible plans (Thompson 1993, p. 24).

Q   If the tax subsidy is lost, will it be worthwhile to retain a flexible benefits plan?

A   Retaining flexes will depend on the value to your company and to the employees. This cannot be measured only in terms of dollars and cents, although cost is surely an important consideration. Surveys suggest that benefits are important to employees and if your employees highly value a flexible plan, it may be worthwhile retaining some features.

Q   Several of our employees want to know if they could go to a cancer screening being offered by a local academic health center. Since we offer a flexible benefits plan, wouldn't that be a good item to include? The cost is $45.

A   For a comprehensive cancer screening, especially for those employees 50 years of age and over, those in high-risk families, or for determining risk, screening is an excellent use of an expense item under the flexible benefits program. Encourage it. It is an advantage of a flexible benefits program.

Q   How can I decide what to retain and what to eliminate in our current flexible plan?

A   Use one of several strategies to get information from your employees. Try focus group discussions, quality circles, or a simple survey to obtain employee preferences. It would be helpful to have an assessment of where the company and your own CEO are going prior to this information gathering.

Q   When we assess for a flexible benefits plan, are there keys to the assessment? What are the more important ones?

A   Stay with the two keys to quality which are financial stability and customer service (Thompson 1992, p. 24). The insurers who can provide these will survive.

Q   If we continue to offer as many flexible benefits as we have in the past, our package will be impossible to manage. How can we achieve a balance?

A   Find out how important options are to your employees in general. Then, if you stay with options, stay with their top one or two.

Q   How viable are the flexible benefits plans?

A   Predictions vary, but many suggest that the more highly flexible benefits plans will not survive. If tax cuts are eliminated, then their viability will also be limited.

TYPES OF FLEXIBLE PLANS

Q   We are exploring a modular plan. What are the advantages of this plan?

A   A *modular plan* is a type of approach for flexible benefits. In contrast to a totally flexible plan, the modular gives choices in certain areas or modules. An advantage for the company is that a modular plan is less difficult to design and implement. Employee decisions are more limited and therefore simpler to administer (Foster 1986).

Q What are the disadvantages of a modular plan?

A While they have attractive features, the modular offers fewer choices and thus employees may feel they are making compromises in their choices. It has less flexibility which may contradict the original intent of the flexible benefits plan (Foster 1986).

Q We are not at all sure we want to shift to a flexible benefits plan. Would a spending account be a good alternative?

A It might be. A *flexible spending account* (FSA) is a mini-flexible device. Some directors use it as a first step. Employees are credited each year with an account for dollars they may spend on selected benefit options (Foster 1986).

Q Where does the money come from for an FSA?

A In the past it has come from one of two sources: the employees' own money or the employer. If it is the employees' money it is usually pretax money (Foster 1986).

Q An employee wants to use her money for dental care but we cover dental care. Can she use it for that?

A Probably not. The three types of coverage for the FSA include items not covered by the employer, legal services for a group, or for a dependent care plan (Foster 1986). If you cover dental, this employee will need to cover another item.

Q   Can an employee get cash if it is not all used in the FSA?

A   No. If, at the end of the specified time—a year—there is money unused in the FSA it may not be credited to the employee or returned in cash (Foster 1986).

Q   An employee of ours used an FSA at a different company. She was upset because she had to pay taxes on the returned cash. Is this right?

A   No and yes. In the early years of the FSA, because the cash amount is set aside or put into the FSA as a credit, pretax dollars were used. If, however, that amount is unused and returned to the employee it must be taxed. However, the IRS frowned on the system; now the employee either uses it or loses it. This needs to be explained to employees so they choose a dollar amount very close to projected reality.

Q   Can an employee roll over the amount not used?

A   No. The amount selected is put in and is lost if unused; it cannot be "rolled over" into the next year. It was originally thought this would be the case, but this feature was discontinued (Foster 1986).

Q   Our CEO wants to have a highly flexible benefits plan for the high-level managers and administrators in our company. Other employees would not have this type of plan. I say this would be too unwieldy. Do other firms do this?

A   Such differentiation is decreasing in popularity. The more egalitarian forms of management suggest this is a less wise choice among firms. What are the tradeoffs in terms of image and employee–employer relations? These may outweigh the flex advantage for management.

Q   We want to encourage employees to select a less expensive form of coverage and use an HMO. Can an FSA or a flexible account do that?

A   Yes. If the employee has a set amount to spend, say $300 per year, and elects to use an HMO, obviously that amount—the $300—will go further than with the traditional fee-for-service delivery model.

Q   Can we have both a set plan and a menu plan?

A   While this is possible, it may be a more complex option than you want to offer. A question for you to consider is the size of your company and the number of employees benefitted in relation to the support needed to administer both a set and a menu plan. Usually, a company shifts from a set to a menu, although it is possible to do the opposite.

Q   Are there advantages of a set plan over a menu?

A   From the vantage point of the company, the set plan offers less in benefits and is less cumbersome to administer. In contrast, the menu plan is attractive to employees and is gaining in preference among company employees. If you are going to delete a large proportion of your prior options within a set plan, shifting to a menu may deflect attention from this cutback. Employees see a menu as attractive.

Q   Is a combination plan the best package?

A   A combination plan is more complex to administer, may take more support services, and will require more human resource commitment. While employees may see it as an advantage, the company needs to assess the combination in comparison to either a set or a menu plan. In most instances, one or the other is a more appropriate move, especially for a relatively small company.

Q Why do employees prefer menu plans?

A A current issue in health care reform and in benefits is choice; in particular, the ability of consumers, including your employees, is to retain a choice of selection for their physicians. For this reason, a menu gives employees choice in their health care benefits, including also some choice about provider.

Q What is the difference between a cafeteria plan and a flexible benefits plan?

A One might think of a cafeteria plan as a type of flexible benefits plan. A cafeteria plan lets the consumer select from several options. The larger the cafeteria, the larger the menu! It is a kind of flexible benefit; the key is the tax advantage it offers.

Q A representative group of our employees met with those of us working in the benefits office last week. The employees wanted to change from the traditional Blue Cross–Blue Shield type of coverage to a preferred provider group. They said this type of offering retained a lot of customer–patient choice. Is this true?

A Yes. Although a preferred provider group consists of physicians joined to offer services, the customer has a choice in whom the primary physician will be. There is no assignment of a primary physician as there is with a health maintenance organization. Remember, in the absence of the chosen physician, another one will offer services as a backup. However, this would be true of any service.

CHANGES IN HEALTH CARE BENEFITS

Q   What should we anticipate in the health care future so that we can remain flexible?

A   More emphasis on prevention, more on health in contrast to illness; any model effective in the delivery of care while retaining or approximating quality, and holding costs steady. If you develop this effective single model, go public!

Q   Do we need to use second opinions?

A   Yes, in most instances they are a prevention against escalating charges and, therefore, increased cost reimbursement. As a safeguard, they are wise, but may not always be required.

Q   How do I match our company's coverage plan to our employees?

A   Use your claims from the past and information from your employees to tailor a plan that best suits the employee profile.

Q   What is a company employee profile?

A   This is a data picture of your employees. As a human resource director you would benefit from having such information at your fingertips. For example, it could include demographics such as the mean age and age range, the number and type of dependents on average with variance highlighted, and the type of position and length of employment. Your interest in a profile for benefits is not just employment record, but the record of employment matched with benefits used, claims processed, and those items in which the employees are interested in using and retaining.

Q An Hispanic employee came into my office last week and was concerned that employees may not have as much choice about their physicians as they did in the past. In particular, she was concerned that a doctor who spoke Spanish would not be available. What can we do?

A In an age of health care reform, no one will have as much choice as in the past. However, in order to ensure language-appropriate services, most HMOs and group practices—which is the direction in which many companies are moving—do provide such services. Before you finalize the contractual agreements, inquire about these services.

Q Don't some plans in health care delivery provide more options than others?

A Yes. Within health maintenance organizations in general, you have a choice of several providers and services. Because there is a group of providers, there is built-in selection. Range of choice will be contingent upon the size of the organization.

Q Provide suggestions of strategies that other companies are using to cut health care benefits costs and remain flexible. What are the strategies?

A Realize that strategies need to be tailored to your individual company and its particular set of employees. Given that warning, there are several current trends companies are exploring. They include such strategies as cost-sharing through higher deductibles and larger copayments for the employees; more emphasis on utilization reviews which survey all claims and reimbursements; and an increasing emphasis on the managed-care (see Chapter 5) service delivery models. Another is the use of incentives to encourage employee health as well as rewards for health-oriented employees.

Q We have a number of relatively young employees, both men and women, who have preschool children. They want child care as a benefit. What can we do for them if we cut our flex plan?

A Use your assessment to decide. First, get information on the importance for those employees in terms of how willing they might be to give up something else, with the understanding not all employees get all choices; obtain numbers of employees affected by this, especially in terms of inconvenience and travel. Will employees miss more work and be late more often without it? Then, assess the bottom line in terms of dollars, especially since child care in the company is a tax writeoff, and compare this to the cost of offering it. You have the data for a fairly firm decision.

Q We have been thinking of a type of plan which would match the coverage to the employee: Let the employee select what he or she wants. We are a relatively large company and can do so at this time. Is this realistic?

A Choice is a wonderful option for your employees if you can do it. You may want to assess the costs for now and project them over the next five- and ten-year period. There is some concern about the ability to offer such a wide range of selections into the next decade, and into the twenty-first century. Watch for changes in flexible benefits.

Q We are planning to purchase a really inexpensive plan, but I worry about the future. What about inexpensive plans?

A While a plan may be cost-effective right now, the key is the future. What will rate increases be over the next ten years?

I would negotiate a rate-increase ceiling to cap your rate increases, or at minimum get their insurer's rating philosophy. Some companies sell low to attract customers, then raise rates at the next renewal period at an accelerated pace (Thompson 1992, p. 18).

Q We are moving to a more flexible benefits package but within an HMO-type service. We now find our employees do not want this service. What can I do?

A Before making any other changes, find out what the employees object to and assess in light of that information.

Q Our company has always prided itself on having a large group of dedicated and professional employees. However, as we go through this process of health care benefits changes I find our employees are not very professional. They want someone to tell them what to do. Why is this?

A A director of human resources needs to remember the use and implementation of health care is basically an emotionally charged situation. Nothing is more valued in society than health.

Q Is it true that the choice of a health care provider is one of the most difficult that people make?

A Absolutely. It is also one of the most important.

Q It seems to me when we combine the issue of medicine with the issue of choice, we have a really hot topic. Am I right?

A Yes, and one of the most critical that any individual makes, employee or not.

Q I have been amazed at the reactions of our employees to the discussion of moving to a managed-care service from a flex plan. The employees seem to have no flexibility! I thought it was a wise move, or isn't it?

A   It probably is, especially from a financial point of view for the company. Determine what is at the base of the reaction and plan based on that information. Remember, employees value choice in health care.

Q   Although we want to be more flexible in our approach to health care, as the director of our benefits program I am concerned it may end up being more expensive. We have over 1,000 employees, but I am still concerned. What can we do?

A   As a relatively large company, you have the numbers to make a flexible benefits plan work. However, it can be expensive, contingent on what you place on the menu. Limiting the range of choice may be the cost-effective answer.

Q   We are considering including dental care in a new plan and shifting to a more flexible type of coverage. Is this an efficient way to change?

A   Although dental care is an attractive offering, it may place stress on the overall system as it expands a well-used coverage. Assess the cost by adding dental but limiting other ranges a bit more. Use prior claims in both areas as a means of making a final decision.

Q   Although our employees are fairly pleased with their new HMO, several have reported to me that it has almost no flexibility. I thought HMOs were relatively flexible, or am I wrong?

A   A lot depends on what the employees mean by flexibility and what flexibility they expected. In most HMOs there is a list or roster of physicians. While employees may choose a doctor, they are usually assigned to a primary physician. If the primary provider is not available a substitute is used. However, HMOs do not allow a subscriber to simply come in and select a physician visit by visit.

Q   If an employee does not like a particular physician in an HMO, can he or she get another?

A   Yes. This is an advantage of belonging to an HMO. There is some flexibility inherent in the system; the flexibility increases with size. If a patient-employee does not like the primary physician, there are other physicians in the HMO facility, and the larger the facility, the more physicians there are from which to select. However, in most instances such a change does require a request in writing and a fairly good reason. Be prudent in changing, as the same physician may serve as a backup in some future health care situation.

Q   Recently, I received a call from the wife of our CEO. She was irate when she went to the HMO to which we belong. She was told: "Don't call us, we'll call you when your lab work is completed." Since she wanted to know about the results sooner, she called me. Is this typical? I thought they were more flexible.

A   You can imagine how many telephone calls an HMO would receive in any given day if all consumers called in to check on their lab work. It sounds like prudent advice. Most health care facilities will deliver the same message but some may do so in a more tactful manner. Check other HMOs in your area for comparison.

Q   We are a member of a small business group in a rural area. We would really like to be more flexible and have more options in our health care benefits, but we do not have the resources to do that. Is there anything we can do?

A   Yes. Talk with other companies, larger and even smaller, in your region. See what they are doing about their health care benefits. Several companies have joined together to purchase services in a form called an *alliance*. An alliance increases the range of options that can be purchased, especially by a smaller company which you describe. Use the small business group to assist you in negotiating.

Q   Although our employees want flexibility and want to retain some choice, it seems to me that our benefits office is bending over backward to meet their needs. They, however, do not seem very negotiable; most want to retain their current plan and as much choice as possible. Is this typical of the average employee?

A   Yes. Choice in selection of physicians is a very high priority for most consumers and for your employees. Next in line is, of course, the cost. However, you might explore what is at stake in the change you anticipate. Perhaps an HMO with some selection can be a cost-efficient step. Or, a limited range with some choice.

Q   As it happens we have a young work force, which means a lot of our employees have young children. We need to match the coverage we will offer to employee groupings. How can we best do that?

A   Determine the employees' priorities if going with their preference is an option. However, given the numerous routine physicals and immunizations required by the young child population, perhaps a prepaid service such as a health maintenance organization, or, a preferred provider group would be best. The decision may lie in the actual number of children and the other claims among the entire employee group.

Q   Some of our employees want to combine plans. We tend to have a few employees who transfer from one site to another who remain covered. But, they do not get the same services in all the different places. What is the best approach in this situation?

A   A lot depends on the service demand. But, a basic underlying coverage which is fairly comprehensive, like a health maintenance organization plus some options for referral, may be best. Explore also the possibility to negotiate for coverage with an HMO in the various regions on a contingency basis.

REFERENCES

Foster, R. 1986. *The Manager's Guide to Employee Benefits*. New York: Facts on File.

Piacentini, J., and Foley, J. 1992. *EBRI Databook on Employee Benefits, 2nd ed*. Washington, D.C.: Employee Benefits Research Institute.

Thompson, R. 1992. How to buy health insurance. *Nation's Business*, October: 16–20.

Thompson, R. 1993. Health-reform watch. *Nation's Business*, July: 24–25.

7

Retaining Employees with Health Care Benefits

Although it is not always considered a primary retainment feature, health care benefits as a valued commodity have been more frequently placed on the list of ways to retain valued employees. With the numerous changes occurring in health care, strategies to retain employees also change. The health care benefits package offers the astute director of human resources options for assisting his or her company in the retainment and motivation of desirable employees. The benefits package remains one of the most attractive features of many job opportunities and is often a final negotiating point with a sought-after employee. This chapter describes how strategies can be developed to hire good employees and retain them, and to motivate current employees. Health care benefits are a key to the employee pool.

Q   Will health care benefits help me to retain employees?

A   Absolutely. Even in the face of cuts and health care reform which businesses are facing today, health care is an essential employment retention feature. An increasing number of employees are recognizing the high value placed on health care benefits.

Q   How can benefits in health care, especially during cost containment, assist our company in retaining employees?

A   First of all, employees value health care benefits. The more the need for coverage, of course, the greater the value of the coverage. Second, they can be built-in as part of a total package.

Q   What are some ways in which health care benefits can be viewed as a health incentive?

A   Your perspective as an employer is to contain, if not reduce, the costs of your company's benefits coverage for your employees. Thus, the lower the number and amount of claims, the greater the benefit to your company. With that in mind, aim to use the package as an incentive to cut the number, and certainly the amount, of claims.

Q   What specifically can a company do to enhance health care benefits as incentives?

A   Assess what it is the company desires to emphasize and target incentives to address them. For example, if the assessment targets the prevention of disease, then reimburse or plan for a program targeting the incentive. One way the benefits package becomes an incentive is through the tailoring of deductible amounts, offerings, or costs as rewards for healthy behaviors like annual checkups or other preventive measures. These preventive and healthy behaviors are increasingly popular in health care reform.

Q   What can a company do to decrease the fear that "big brother" is watching over employees, which is a relatively common concern among employees today?

A   You are accurate that the word is out that positive changes in lifestyle, such as smoking, eating patterns, or other lifestyle features, are desired by a company. However, the intersection between work and private life is a sensitive one. Without stepping over the boundary into employees' private lives, one solution is to ask workers to sign a company statement indicating whether they engage in a certain behavior. However, select behaviors assessed objectively like weight loss. A company cannot be held responsible for what an employee does while not at work, especially if a signed statement is available. In terms of your insurers, these actions indicate good intentions on the part of the company.

Q   What should I do if I see an employee smoking who has told me he or she does not smoke?

A   Prevention is the best strategy. The human resource director needs to let all employees know, in writing, what will happen in the case of an infringement. For example, you can state in the case noted above where an administrator sees an employee engaging in behavior contrary to what he or she stated, that written information to that effect will need to be included in the company record. A company policy noting you will not, and cannot, look the other way is needed at the same time you make the changes in the benefits package. Potential increases in benefits should be an adequate incentive.

Q One of my employees is giving serious consideration to taking another job with a competing company. She is an executive in a position I would hate to see vacated; she would be difficult to replace. The key issue for her is the health care coverage provided for her and for her family. We anticipate cuts in the future. What can I do for her now?

A A lot depends on the projected benefits plan of your company. The company might decide, for example, the planned reductions need to be tailored to specifics among your employees, such as seniority, or level of position in the company. However, that, too, needs to be carefully thought out. Nevertheless, if your company package recognizes and rewards company loyalty, this executive could retain—as an incentive and reward—a benefits package covering her and her family.

Q Several of my employees have dropped by lately to discuss their concerns about quality of care. None of them are very specific in terms of what they mean by quality of care, or about health care quality. Just what do employees mean when they talk about quality of care?

A In terms of your own employees it would be hard to say specifically. However, for most employees today the concept or term of quality refers to retaining some choice in the health care market. For others it still means choice, but it refers directly to their ability to retain choice in the selection of their own personal or individual health care provider.

Q How does one go about anticipating health care needs?

A No one can precisely predict with a high degree of accuracy, the next decade's health care needs. We do know workers will need immunizations, have colds, and require checkups. Some employees will become ill, but specific illnesses will be difficult to predict. What is important to have is a fairly general idea of what to expect in terms of your claims and what you want to support and reward.

Q   One of my employees who has been with our company for a number of years came into my office last week. He was concerned about his health care and stated he was increasingly worried that, at his age, he was going to have to start to be concerned about even having health care benefits. He stated he never thought our company would let him down. What can I say to an employee with this concern?

A   Unless you have a specific plan in place or on the drawing board, do not promise something you might not deliver. However, it would seem appropriate to respond to the feeling the company has abandoned this employee. The underlying theme is the sense he has been let down and the company has reneged on an earlier promise to cover his health care benefits. Use national data to counter this perception. To address these concerns place this situation in light of the reform changes today, as well as changes occurring for all employees. One assumes his situation is not unique, although his reaction or perception may be relatively unique. A conversation may allay his fears, which should include a reality check on his perceived concerns.

Q   Is there some way we can tailor our benefits package or make it more nuanced in terms of the variety of employees we have? For instance, we have several long-term employees with years of seniority. In contrast, the majority of our employees are quite young. What can we do to address all of their needs?

A   What is called a menu may be the best solution for your particular company. Remember, however, not even a menu package would cover all the needs of each employee. Take into consideration your categories of employees, the numbers of employees in each group, and the options you can realistically offer.

Q   We do not want to lose the productivity our company has built up over these past five or so years. We have gained a lot of momentum in the last several years, after earlier years of real downturn. What can we do from the benefits side of the equation to retain momentum?

A   Are certain employees more productive than others, or are all of your employees productive? Are they productive as a group? If they are productive as individuals, then reward their individuality. With each increase in productivity, expand what the company pays in benefits including health care; reduce the deductible they pay, for example.

If, on the other hand, they are productive as a group, then reward teamwork. Let each team compete for a benefit it values—paid time in the gym, or jogging at lunch. Tailor your reward through your benefits package to what you want to create in outcomes.

Q   I hear from an inside source that several of our best employees are beginning to shop around in terms of health care benefits. What can I do to keep them from shopping?

A   The first solution is to realize you cannot keep employees from shopping around, any more than a physician can keep patients from comparing prices or customers asking about the price of a dress or cost of a tie. Once you have that well in mind, change your attitude. Get aggressive in a positive way and alert employees to the fact that your company will be competitive in the health care benefits market.

Q   What else can I do to be more proactive?

A   There are a number of strategies you could use to be more proactive, especially with your more productive and valued employees. For instance, you might have a special meeting to discuss health care benefits. Or, you could put out announcements to diffuse anger or gossip about cuts. The word is out that cuts are in so you are better off being proactive about the obvious.

Q   One of my employees, who might be called a health care fanatic, came in to tell me he is really not interested in having surgery and such options covered in his package. He really wants just health-oriented choices. What can I do?

A   If you offer a menu, show him and encourage him to select those items on his package. Depending on his age, you might also offer a word of counsel: Most individuals change their minds in the middle years—at about age 45.

Q   Do companies reward healthy eating?

A   I assume that you are referring to the difficulty in knowing whether a person really eats in a healthy manner or not. Since you cannot find out if a person eats well, go by other factors such as appropriate weight which can be obtained objectively through a health care checkup.

Q   What if I find out the variety of choice our employees want in benefits is too great? What then?

A   No company can cover all the choices or wants of employees. However, you can certainly aim toward some middle road and give the majority of the employees what they would like. If you do offer a menu, see what the large minority wants and add it as an option.

Q   I am concerned we might be liable for the reduction of some coverage. Are we?

A   It may depend on the coverage, but if you treat all employees in a fair and consistent manner you should not be liable for reductions in benefits.

Q   Are there some companies considered good places to work?

A   An article called *"The 100 Best Places to Work in America"* lists companies and the features which make them attractive (Reinolds 1993, p. 5F). Of interest to the human resource director is the fact that pay and benefits are high among the list of features considered.

Q   We want to make sure we retain our employees when our company implements a new health care benefits plan. What can we do now to ensure this objective?

A   Find out what is most valued by your employees. Aim for the package based on your cost assessment.

Q   What, in general, are the most important features of a health insurance plan for most employees?

A   According to surveys, most employees state the benefits covered (47 percent) and the monthly premium for their plan (42 percent) are the most important features in valuing their company's health benefits plan (Thompson 1993b, p. 77).

Q   What direction do you think we should go in as a company to keep employees satisfied?

A   Given three choices, 72 percent of workers in small businesses responding to a survey on health insurance stated they preferred their current plan, while 21 percent preferred a national health insurance plan that would be federally financed. Only 7 percent selected the third choice which was a federally mandated play-or-pay plan (Thompson 1993b).

Q We encourage our employees to give us information so we can plan a benefits program that will keep them satisfied. Our plan is one of the only options we have to encourage and retain our employees. However, I also see that employees do a lot of changing around when they have options. Is this typical of most, and if so, what are the data on changing?

A When asked if they have changed health care plans in the past five years, workers in relatively small companies reply affirmatively (Thompson 1993b). Among those responding, only 28 percent have not changed, whereas 19 percent have changed three or more times; 27 percent changed once and 26 percent changed twice. It seems that workers are, indeed, shopping around.

Q We think one key to retaining employees is our excellent retirement benefits package. Do other companies use their benefits package to retain employees, or, are we on track since benefits are so expensive?

A Given the current figures on employee coverage, I would say you are on target. For example, in 1990 only 42 percent of all American employees were covered by a health care plan in retirement (Thompson 1993a, p. 58). That figure is projected to decrease.

Q We think a worker's compensation package would keep our employees satisfied, but we also think it is too expensive. Where are other companies doing in terms of worker's compensation?

A   Given the fact the worker's comp industry has not shown a profit in over 20 years, it is an expensive venture. It is also an area hard hit by changes. However, it is still an attractive feature to employees.

Q   My CEO wants to become much more stringent about the amount of coverage we offer our employees. As the director of human resources, I hear the daily stories of these employees, and I think the decision is a mistake. While we may need to trim, I think continuing to offer some kind of health care package is an asset to our company and keeps us on the competitive edge. Which is right, or are we both wrong?

A   No one wants to be caught in an argument between a human resource director and a boss, but you both have a point. Health care is escalating, but employees value it. It does give you an edge. For example, 36.3 million Americans were uncovered by health insurance in 1991 (Thompson 1993a, p. 58). These figures represent a decline in a valued commodity, because in 1988 only 33.6 million were uncovered; it is central to health care reform.

Q   As a large company we are distressed because we are about to lose several of our best employees. Yesterday, two of my best workers announced they are leaving because of better health care benefits at a competing company. What can we do?

A   Start with a frank conversation with the two employees. Of key interest is how satisfied they are with your company. While there is an inevitable turnover among employees, it is difficult to lose good workers for issues over which you have control. Given the type of package you offer, is there some flexibility in what you can counter-offer?

Q   If an assessment does not provide any useful information, what else can I do? My boss is really unhappy.

A   Just what do these competing companies offer that you do not? Find out from these two employees. In particular, are the two workers after the same benefits or are there different issues for each?

Q   We are changing our benefits and I already anticipate that we may lose several employees. What can I do to avoid this? I am not looking forward to telling my boss that benefits changes encouraged them to leave.

A   Did your boss encourage you to reduce benefits, or did your company offer a choice? Get your boss on your side first. Then, assess the employees.

Q   We would like to start offering a more comprehensive package of health care in anticipation of changes. In terms of employee retention, what would be the best direction to go?

A   A lot will depend on the work force you have and their age. A number of young children as dependents would suggest child care or a prepaid plan, for example. On the other hand, highly professional employees particularly like the flexibility of a flex plan. Determine the work force and then plan accordingly. Explore this with an employees' benefits group.

Q   We want to expand our offerings and at the same time increase our attractiveness as a company for retaining our present work force. In addition, our CEO is exploring writeoffs on taxes. Wouldn't programs we offer to enhance health care or wellness be the best way to go?

A   Programs can be writeoffs, however, you might need to demonstrate use. Several companies have successfully implemented walking or jogging, aerobics, weight-reduction programs, stress alerts (and reduction), a healthy office, and Eat Right programs. You can combine any of these into a successful and efficient wellness program.

Q   Do we need to offer health care programming on-site to get a tax credit for it?

A   It is clearer for the purposes of argument for your position if you do, but check with a tax consultant on that one. You do not want an IRS infringement. It may depend on the company and the site.

Q   How can we think through retaining employees by using health care benefits?

A   Start by assessing what the high priorities are for your employees, or better yet, for groups of employees. Explore what can be obtained in your area or near to your company facility. Creative options may be available in your company's area you can purchase, or purchasing in combination with a more modest offering. For example, if there is an HMO you may get the comprehensive coverage you desire and also fit the preference of a large number of employees. Then you can add something else for retainment purposes.

Q   What are companies doing in terms of combinations?

A   One example is a company offering reductions in costs if the employees are willing to purchase generic drugs at cost savings. These savings are significant dollar figures for both large and small companies.

Q   I think we are too serious at work. I have been thinking about building in some fun, humor, and health-oriented programs. Does this seem off the wall?

A Not according to reports on good places to work (Reinolds 1993, p. 5F). Positive work environments include laughter and humor. Use them to enhance productivity as well as the retention of your employees.

Q What is known about the organizational culture in terms of health care benefits?

A Although there is no known link between the company's or organization's culture and benefits, it is known that a positive culture has explicit norms and expectations and higher productivity among the companies' employees (McDaniel and Stumpf 1993, p. 54). Use the health care benefits to enhance your company's culture by directly linking the benefits and their rewards, with aims of the company and making them explicit to the employees. You will enhance the organization's culture.

WELLNESS AND EMPLOYEE ASSISTANCE PROGRAMS

Q What is the key difference between a wellness program and an employee assistance program (EAP)?

A A wellness program aims to promote a healthy lifestyle, whereas the employee assistance programs provide referral or counseling on specific issues such as substance abuse and alcoholism, marital difficulties, emotional problems, or family and legal problems (U.S. Dept. of Labor 1992, p. 68).

Q Of the two, the wellness and the employee assistance programs, which is the more popular?

A   Although both are growing in popularity, the assistance programs are offered by about two times as many employers (Piacentini and Foley 1992).

Q   Our firm has more than 600 employees. We are thinking of offering a wellness program but we are not sure if this is the right direction. Given the expense of such programs we are questioning this direction. What do similar companies in our size range offer?

A   Among private companies of medium and large size offering health care benefits for their full-time employees, about 23 percent offer wellness programming of some type (Piacentini and Foley 1992).

Q   Is the data similar for smaller firms?

A   No. Smaller firms tend not to have as many options among their full-time employee benefits, including wellness programs.

Q   My boss thinks because we are a computer program and service firm with a large number of younger employees, a wellness program would be popular with them and would assist in employee retention. Is this true?

A   Apparently. If you look at the statistics on wellness programs, the professional employee group is the one that uses it the most. For example, in government data on full-time workers in large firms, professional employees elected to use wellness programs twice as much as production and service personnel (Piacentini and Foley 1992).

Q   For retention purposes it would seem to us a program emphasizing health promotion and wellness would be much more attractive than an employee assistance type of program. However, it seems that among my colleagues more of their companies offer assistance than promotion. Is this true?

A   The numbers show assistance programs in all types of firms are available almost twice as often as health promotion or wellness programs (Piacentini and Foley 1992).

Q   We are a moderate-sized firm affiliated with a local government agency. Because of this affiliation we offer similar benefits packages to those the government offers. What are the trends in the government-related firms regarding wellness or assistance programs?

A   Among government-related agencies, there is a tendency to offer more employee assistance programs than wellness programs (Piacentini and Foley 1992). This is a trend similar to one found in other private firms. However, there is greater emphasis on assistance programs in the government sector in general.

Q   We assume many employers need to offer the assistance programs, whereas, the wellness promotion programs may be less essential. Is this accurate?

A   Although both have attractive features, it is accurate employers have a more direct mandate to provide assistance programs including the program's help with substance abuse. In contrast, the wellness and health promotion programs emphasizing a healthy lifestyle are more in line with retention and recruitment of employees.

Q   Is it true wellness and employee assistance programs are attractive to employees?

A   Yes. Both of these program types are growing in importance to employees.

Q   We think that offering child care for our employees will help us keep employees. Is this accurate?

A   Yes. Although it has shown slow growth there is a positive trend for more child-care programs. As the demographics of the work force change, and with an increase in two-worker households, there is an increasing emphasis on quality child care (U.S. Dept. of Labor 1992, p. 68).

Q   What other types of programming are small firms using to recruit and retain their good employees? We need some creative suggestions.

A   The widest variety of programs is offered by larger firms. Transportation benefits are offered by the vast majority of smaller firms, about 85 percent of them. Among smaller firms nonproduction bonuses or discounts are also popular, as well as education-related programs that enhance the employees' competency.

Q   Is it accurate that nonjob-related benefits are seldom offered in today's economy?

A   By and large this is accurate. Among firms of all sizes, educational benefits pertain to the job or job skills (Piacentini and Foley 1992).

Q   How do these offerings differ for smaller firms?

A   Among those private smaller firms that offer benefits, around 10 percent offer some educational benefit (Piacentini and Foley 1992).

Q   Is it true most small firms do not even consider nonjob-related offerings?

A The proportions between offerings in education that relate to the job and those that do not are clearly more differentiated in the small private companies. For example, in the early 1990s, while 10 percent offered education benefits related to their job for full-time employees, only 1 percent offered nonjob-related benefits (Piacentini and Foley 1992).

Q We have a large number of production employees and very few professional ones. We think it would not be wise to venture into educational benefits. Is this correct?

A It probably is, although each company needs to assess educational offerings in light of its current and projected needs regarding training and support. Education can be an attractive employee feature. In terms of data, of firms offering an educational benefit only 6 percent offered it to production workers.

Q Was the proportion of professionals offered educational benefits significantly larger?

A In contrast to production or technical and clerical workers, employees in the professional category obtained educational benefits more often than any other type of employee. In 1990 it was available to 18 percent of full-time employees in small private firms (Piacentini and Foley 1992).

Q Our firm has less than 100 employees and is eager to establish several new benefits that will be attractive to our employees and give us more of an edge in our increasingly competitive community. Which benefits should we consider?

A Among the full-time employees in smaller firms, the benefits offered tend to be benefits discounts and some form of transportation benefits, usually either free or subsidized parking for workers (Piacentini and Foley 1992).

Q   Ds these data reflect what is offered or what employees selected? We want to compare our options with other firms.

A   Data provided in reports reflect information about those employees who are eligible for certain offerings. The report does not differentiate between items desired by employees, and those offered by the company. A survey would need to be tailored to a specific firm to solicit information on what employees desired. One would assume, however, when offered a benefit option employee selection would be reflected in those data on what is actually used.

Q   We have been wondering if it would be prudent to begin to offer an on-site infirmary for minor injuries or some screening. Is this a smart direction in which to move?

A   It may well be. However, the size of your company will probably be a factor. Among small firms there are relatively few in-house infirmaries (Piacentini and Foley 1992).

Q   We have over 200 employees and want to begin more screening for injuries on the job by getting base-line screens to use for prevention and comparison. Base-line screening and physicals can be used to establish a base to which future changes can be compared; it will assist in ruling out prior illnesses or injuries, for example. Base-line screening can also be used to validate the attainment of incentives. For example, if employees are encouraged to lose weight, a base-line weight can determine successful attainment of a target weight for which a lower deductible amount may be offered by our company to the employees. We can use an infirmary service to do this. Will this work?

A   Yes, and it fits with the offerings in health care benefits for medium- to large-sized firms such as yours. An in-house infirmary is a benefit for 40 percent of all types of employees in these firms (Piacentini and Foley 1992).

Q   We think that it might be attractive to employees to offer an in-house infirmary, since health care is so expensive. Can this be an effective way to reduce costs?

A   It might be, but you would need to specify what services an in-house infirmary would offer. Most employers do not want to be in the business of providing health care services. Make a careful assessment, but do consider that an infirmary does offer a valued commodity that may assist in retaining valued employees, and for some less expensive and perhaps initial screening services for employees.

Q   What can we do to balance the attractive features with cost and efficiency?

A   Hire a certified nurse practitioner to staff the service. Practitioners are a very cost-effective way to offer quality service which is designed for medical management, some diagnosis and initial screening, particularly focused on the relatively low-risk consumer. More risky or difficult employees can be referred to an appropriate source.

Q   Are there other features that employees find attractive that would make our company more competitive? We are willing to invest in some new benefits programs related to health care.

A   What about the family leave which is a federally mandated benefit? Building into your benefits program some specific features to support employees who need to take leave for parental care, an ill spouse, or for themselves, such as a support group for getting back to work, and how to design and implement a successful leave, can be an attractive employee feature.

Q What exactly do employees find difficult pertaining to family leaves?

A There are issues of reentry into the work force, especially if the leave was taken by the employee for him- or herself. In addition, if there are job changes, even though an equivalent job may be available, the additional stress of returning to the work force in a relatively new situation or position can be a critical factor in the successful return and reentry of these employees.

Q Could we use support groups to keep track of employees and build in the support as a retention feature?

A Why not? The law on family leave states employers have the option of requesting updated information regarding the intentions and leave status of workers on leave and this, too, can be designed into a support group or communication system for employees. Continuing communication builds better employee–employer relations which is an enhancement feature for the company. For efficiency, make your programs serve more than one purpose.

Q We are a company with a relatively high risk service. We employ window washers as well as construction workers. We find our employees take our training program which is quite good, work a short while, then leave. We think we would be able to retain more employees with a better health care benefits program. What if we offered more disability insurance?

A   In your firm, disability is clearly a factor. In addition to the Social Security Old-Age and Survivors Insurance Program which covers almost all workers, the Supplemental Security Income (SSI) is available for those between the ages of 21 and 64. However, given the rising costs in health care, many workers are concerned that disability insurance may become prohibitive. A complementary program, therefore, would be an attractive employee option.

Q   If we move ahead with this benefits feature, what can we say to our employees who think the solvency of the social security system is in question? Is solvency a relevant question?

A   Yes. There are projections of potential insolvency for the Social Security Old-Age and Survivors Insurance (OASI) trust fund ". . . the middle of the next century" (Piacentini and Foley 1992).

Q   Is the projection for the OASI trust fund a conservative estimate or not?

A   A projection for an estimated date around the middle of the twenty-first century should reassure most current employees. Nevertheless, more conservative estimates use the year 2026 as a projection date (Piacentini and Foley 1992). A supplemental benefit would be a positive retention strategy for your workers.

Q   We know among our current employees raising their copayment and deductible amount will be met with displeasure. On the other hand, we also know payment from employees is fruitful as a preventive device. What is the balance if we want to use our benefits as a complementary retention program?

A   In terms of a dollar amount there is no exact statistic available. However, if you offered to pay slightly more of the employee contribution than the average, or dropped below the traditional 20 percent (matching the 80 percent) copayment amount, surely it keeps you competitive.

Q   What are the critical features of health care cuts and benefits employees seem to be concerned with if we want to shift to a more retention-oriented program?

A   First is continued coverage, and second is the specific amount of the deductible.

Q   We are considering lowering the age at which employees are vested in our pension program. Would this be attractive enough to keep employees?

A   Pension is valued and important for the majority of employees. However, the appeal of a particular feature may depend on the age of an employee. Obviously, the closer one is to retirement the more important retirement becomes. For those over the age of 40 it would probably be quite attractive.

Q   What if we dropped any criteria for vesting? What would dropping do for our retention?

A   The question then becomes whether the firm can afford it and whether vesting should be tied with any longevity. Few companies offer immediate vesting in a pension plan.

Q   Because of the types of service that we offer we tend to attract a number of females. Each year we have more and more women, both with and without dependents. We are thinking a way to retain some of the better employees would be to offer a fully vested pension plan for those particular employees. Would this be appropriate?

A It depends on how you qualify it. If your criteria can be applied across the board, or if you specify certain levels like executive management or administrative positions, then it would be appropriate. However, if you discriminate against certain employees where it is not available on a universal basis you could be cited.

REFERENCES

McDaniel, C., & Stumpf, L. 1993. The organizational culture in nursing services. *The Journal of Nursing Administration* 17(4): 54–60.

Piacentini, J., and Foley, J. 1992. *EBRI Databook on Employee Benefits, 2nd ed.* Washington, D.C.: Employee Benefits Research Institute.

Reinolds, C. 1993. Best U.S. workplaces combine shrewd business with fun. *News & Observer*, 6 June: 5F.

Thompson, R. 1993a. Uninsured population grows. *Nation's Business*, March: 58.

Thompson, R. 1993b. Views on health insurance. *Nation's Business*, January: 77.

U.S. Department of Labor. 1992. *Employee Benefits in a Changing Economy* 2394, September: 68.

8

Rewarding Employees

One of the challenges facing the health benefits administrator is rewarding the employee with health care packaging. This has its positive side as contemporary reforms in health care turn from an emphasis on cure to one of health and wellness. With these in mind, this chapter targets a number of ways in which the creative and proactive director of benefits and resources can tailor the health care benefits package to the individual employee and reward healthy behavior. This chapter will assist you in designing a health benefits package that will retain the healthy worker and reward those behaviors that are not only cost-effective, but healthy for the employee as well as for the company.

PLANNING REWARDS FOR EMPLOYEES

Q We want to emphasize health rather than illness. What can we do to get that point across?

A In the company newsletter or in various communications from your office make it clear health is in and illness is out. A second way is to create a new language in the company. Talk health rather than illness.

Q How does one create a healthy office?

A It is assumed that a healthy office is one in which there are no health hazards or behaviors on the part of employees that endanger the health of other employees. To cite an obvious example, employees may not smoke except in designated areas.

Q We want to reduce the number of sick days our employees take each year. Not only do we want to reduce the number they actually take, but we also want to reduce the number awarded to them. How do we do that?

A You will have to decide whether you want to go cold turkey or phase this in. If you want to go cold turkey, then take all the cuts at one time. Otherwise, a gradual phase-in—or in this case, phase-out—of the numbers of days can be implemented over a one- to three-year period.

  Start by awarding new and incoming employees with the target number and phasing old employees on a schedule so that they may adjust.

Q How can we also reduce the number of sick days employees take?

A You need to decide what number of sick days you want to have as a reward, then implement that number. An innovative approach would be to reward employees who use no or very few sick days with a lower deductible rate on their benefits, for example. Rewards could be portions of a payback or of unused sick time.

Q How can we get the message across?

A Go companywide with your plans and intentions. More important, go companywide with the implementation. When you reward an employee for using the lowest number of sick days in a given year, for instance, highlight it in the company newsletter or an awards banquet. Get the message out there. Get your CEO involved. How many does he or she use?

Q We want to package health. How can we do that?

A Use a marketing approach similar to that which you might use to sell your product. What you want to do for your company's employees is to sell them on health.

Q Some of our employees behave as if they do not care about their health, or they behave in unhealthy ways, like smoking a lot, for example. What can we do to encourage them to change their behavior?

A Not to care about one's health in today's market can be expensive. Actually, you and the company do not really care about your employees' attitude. What you want is a behavior change. You can get the message across by rewarding positive attitudes translating into positive behavior change. It is too expensive for the employee, as well as for the company, to ignore health.

Q What else can we do?

A Attempt to hire employees who care about their health. Gently inquire about their interest in health as it pertains to work. Promote positive-attitude employees, and today, that includes attitudes about health.

Q What about signs in work areas?

A Good question. Even signs can convey a positive health image. Get signs that point the way to the health club as well as signs in the cafeteria on positive dietary habits and food choices. Make sure the company cafeteria offers these healthy options!

Q   What about the pictures employees have or that we allow?

A   Unless the pictures are offensive and a breach of good taste or convey a bias or a prejudice, it would be difficult to make a comment about a particular employee's pictures or posters. However, you as a high-level administrator can set a tone in your office by displaying posters, pictures, or other images as reminders of healthy behaviors you want to encourage. Employees will get the message. Remember: One picture is worth a thousand words!

Q   What about personal pictures?

A   There are CEOs who display pictures of their family conveying messages not only of family togetherness, but of health and vitality depicting their annual ski trip, sailing, or whatever activity they enjoy. Get the active pictures of your family out and display them where anyone coming into the office can see them.

Q   My CEO thinks we need a gym. I say it is too expensive, and we have too few employees who would use it. Am I right?

A   Hard to tell. How many employees do you have? Would your CEO also use a gym? On the other hand, if there is a gym nearby, you might contact it, and arrange a company-sponsored program to encourage employees to attend. Then, if an increasing number become active in the gym, assess whether it is worth it for the company to build or acquire one.

Q   Can you give me an example of a successful program for encouraging employee health?

A   Yes. A current example is the StayWell Program which the Chrysler Corporation just implemented in its Technology Center near Detroit, MI (*Business Week* 1993). According to the administrators, everyone is welcome—from the executives to the janitors.

Q   In this program, what are employees receiving as a health benefit?

A   They receive everything from screening for relatively common health care problems, for instance, blood pressure or excess weight, to low-fat meals in the company cafeteria. In addition, they may attend classes on weight loss and self-defense. There is a range of offerings in a brand new facility with fitness consultants (*Business Week* 1993).

Q   Are there any data on the link between employee productivity and wellness or fitness programs?

A   No more than between jogging and productivity or overall general physical activity and productivity. The link between physical wellness and productivity is well established. What you are actually questioning is the location of the activity, and it does not make a difference in terms of the link. Location does make a difference to employees, especially for ensuring the activity happens on a more routine and daily basis.

Q   We want to get specific about some health care problems we have among our employees. Where do we start?

A   Start at the top in this case. Use your own CEO as an example, and if he or she is not on this one then the first step is a frank discussion with the CEO. The aim here is to get him or her to provide an incentive for employees further down the line. Nothing like a good example at the top. Remember the photos of the president jogging!

Q   Exactly what might a CEO do?

A   It may seem a bit personal, but health and facts and figures about health are not what they used to be a decade ago. And, today, health translates into dollars. For a first step, see if the CEO is willing to go public with some health figures. For example, could he lose ten pounds and tell everyone about it? Or, could he reduce his cholesterol level by 15 points and put it into the newsletter? Even better, why don't you develop a company challenge program: For those employees who are able to lower their cholesterol through dietary change, every one point of cholesterol reduced could be rewarded with a prize. Or reward a reduction in the total amount of fat or salt (sodium) intake in the daily diets of employees. There are numerous possibilities.

Q   It seems to me this thing about health and health care is rather amorphous. What exactly are some target areas?

A   Although health is specific to individuals, there are some generalities that can be discussed. For example, most practitioners recognize that weight, cholesterol, exercise, and smoking are key factors. These health care indicators are, to a certain degree, linked to lifestyle features and can be controlled by employees. That is especially true of weight, smoking, and exercise, but less so of cholesterol which is often genetically influenced. Even so, in some individuals, diet can be a control factor for cholesterol levels.

Q What about stress on the job?

A The jury is still out on the final answer to stress, however there is increasing evidence to suggest that increased amounts of stress, whether at work or in other areas of one's life, can affect immunity levels and the ability to ward off infections.

Q Should we aim to reduce stress?

A Some stress is not only inevitable, but is related to incentives or motivation leading to productivity. If the stress level is perceived to be adversely contributing to the productivity level, then it needs to be addressed.

Q Are there ways we can target stress?

A Aim for stress reducers each employee can use. For example, provide an avenue for jogging or walking at lunch, get employees involved in some informal activities to engage in on work breaks that do not involve smoking or unhealthy eating. Find some healthy substitutes.

Q We also need to reach the families. How can we do that?

A Several ideas come to mind. Why not try something new at the annual company picnic or the annual holiday party? Instead of offering heavy food and alcoholic drinks, emphasize healthy substitutes. When the spouses and family members are present, discuss the company's changing emphasis.

Q What else can we do?

A Why not have an all-family meeting or conference for discussion about health care benefits where they can come and discuss and ask questions? Give them the facts in terms of expense. Although it is changing, women often make health decisions regarding, for example, choice of physicians, as well as appointments for treatment and screening. Also, get to the person who plans and cooks meals. Food and food preparation are usually keys to health change, although others can influence what is purchased and prepared; that influencing person may be your employee!

Q Alas, although I am the human resource director, I am not very health conscious. Is it essential I get involved to convert our office into a more health conscious one?

A Yes. Think of your change in attitude as a health benefit for you in the long run. It will be important to the employees that they do not perceive a mixed message from your company.

HEALTH CARE STRATEGIES

Q What are other companies doing to reward the more healthy employees?

A There are a variety of strategies out there. Some include outright advances in benefits, some are reductions in the deductible, and others include bonuses. However, as with all rewards, you are better to link the reward as directly as possible with the behavior. I would reward the healthy employee with a monetary item translating directly into the benefit. For example, if you do not smoke for one year, or six months, then your deductible will decrease by X percentage points.

Q Can we also change deductibles if we find a change toward unhealthy behavior?

A   Absolutely. You need to tell employees, that if they do not position themselves for healthy behavior, their deductibles will continue to go up, or other similar examples.

Q   Are there creative health programs out there? If so, we would welcome some examples.

A   The number of creative approaches to the healthy employee is expanding exponentially. For example, in addition to the development or purchase of a gym or health club, several companies are going out on their own. They are organizing health fairs, a health week, Health-Wise Employee of the Month, or "best benefit" of the year worker. The options are limitless.

Q   An employee came into my office last week. She was disturbed that we no longer allowed smoking in our company building. This decision was the result of an employee vote last year, and we are now implementing that vote. However, she is a good employee, and except for this outburst she has always been quite a pleasant worker. What can I do to help her become a more health-oriented employee?

A   It would not hurt to remind her of the objective health benefits of quitting smoking, starting with her own health. Then, suggest some alternative activities like walking, a hobby, or other more healthy behaviors. An additional issue for these workers may also be the change in the informal social relationships that occur among friends or peers when they smoke. An activity that allows them to socialize as workers, but over a healthy activity, would be a good alternative: walking or jogging together at lunch, for example.

Q   We seem to have a number of company employees who do not think in terms of health. They continually talk about illness, their diseases, and seem to resist the thought of going for an annual checkup. Is there any way to get them more involved in preventive and positive activities? They are also proving to be somewhat expensive.

A   Through your benefits plan you can reward the type of healthy behaviors that you desire. Then, gradually shift away from rewarding the expensive and unhealthy behaviors. Use the benefits package to shift the employees' attitudes toward rewards tied to the benefits and the employees' contribution to it through better health.

Q   Our employees are unhappy at the prospect of benefits cuts, especially in health care. But given we will cut, there must be some way to motivate them. What are some examples?

A   Why not try an all-company approach and get everyone involved? Bring in a company nurse practitioner and do blood-pressure screening, cholesterol counts, diabetes screening, etc. Make sure that the CEO is there. You could end the day with a 1K run or walk and a large picnic. Give a prize for the best dessert with the fewest calories, for example. If you use this to convert employees and get the higher-level employees and managers involved, it could turn out to be a fun and productive day. Call it a benefits kickoff!

Q   Some companies are talking directly to consumers to see what they like. How could we apply this concept to the employees and health care benefits?

A   Go directly to your employees as consumers for a start. Find out what those employees affected by your insurers would like. Perhaps an open discussion between some selected employees and a health care provider would be an opportunity to not only gain information, but to strengthen a negotiated relationship.

Q   We are getting a lot of complaints about the change in our benefits. In particular, we have received complaints the families we cover can no longer get to the new HMO facility we changed to this past year. How do others address this employee dependent issue?

A   There are a number of ways, but reaching families and dependents to reward the employees is a direct and tailored way to use the benefits program. Plan a specific strategy to reach out to dependents or families.

Q   Because of complaints about the changes in our benefits program, we are thinking about initiating a transportation feature as a part of the program. Do you know of others offering this feature?

A   Most programs are in a cost containment phase and are cutting back. However, it is a creative venture and might enhance your employees' use of preventive aspects of a benefits program. Parking and transfer from parking to the company is commonly offered as an employee benefit.

Q   If we decide to go with transportation, any ideas on how to tailor it?

A   Why not offer it on a sign-up basis and only on certain days? If you want to encourage preventive dimensions in your program and encourage and reward health, then use the transportation offering as a means of getting the employees and their dependents into those programs via the transportation service.

Q   We were thinking of asking dependents to pay a small amount for this transportation service. Do you think this is the way to go?

A   No, as you can use it as a tax write-off. Also, you could more directly reward the employee by putting a savings for prevention into the bonus or directly into a lower deductible. Asking for a contribution, regardless of how small, will probably be counterproductive in the long run. Keep the rewards tied to the aim.

Q   We need some creative ideas to continue to expand our program so we reward our employees. Is it true that some companies are quite creative in this area?

A   Yes, and they have moved directly into preventive measures. The key is to use the rewards to bolster your aim. If the aim is more preventive screening, then use a strategy that rewards that objective: Offer a lower deductible to employees who get an annual screening exam(s).

Q   What other ideas have companies used?

A   Focus on the behavior of employees since you cannot control motivation. For example, if you want to encourage prevention and screening among employees, then reward annual mammograms for the female employees, or for males reward an annual prostate checkup or stress checkups for all employees over age 50.

Q   What about group ventures? We have some who work in groups as teams.

A   This is a good motivating plan; however, you may have some groups with few members, for example, who smoke. Nonsmokers are excluded and therefore at a disadvantage. Think this one through carefully.

Q   What about offering incentives to employees on an individual level? Is this a problem?

A   Not if every employee has an equal opportunity to participate.

Q   Since so few of our employees continue to smoke, I am afraid smoking reduction will not attract enough of our employees. How do we address this issue?

A   Perhaps, like some benefits programs, you can offer an "incentive menu." For example, to cover both smokers and nonsmokers, you could offer a choice of not smoking, losing weight, or increasing exercise.

Q   Couldn't we also offer an incentive for those who have never smoked and to those who quit earlier?

A   Of course. Keep the issue of fairness and justice alive by providing a similar incentive or benefit bonus to all employees. Those who never smoked can receive a bonus for not smoking and are treated equally, for instance, along with those who stop smoking.

Q   We do not do much with health education in our company. I think education would be a good move for our employees, but we do not know where to start. What do other firms do?

A   Education is a good plan and can reach a large number of employees. Begin by setting some objectives for your benefits program. For example, if you want to discourage smoking, plan a smoking program. Keep it short and interesting. An increasing number of companies are building education into their benefits programs.

Q   Are there other educational programs available?

A   There are several good training programs and trainers around. Look into videos that can deliver your message.

Q   Aren't videos costly?

A   Not at all. For companies with several branches, they are a very cost-effective way to reach a number of employees at one time; you can continue to offer it as part of the benefits program.

Q   I have been thinking about a benefits orientation for new employees. Does any company offer a program like that?

A   Work up a company slide presentation or a video with pizazz that can do what you want. A good video can be eyecatching as well as efficient for your personnel.

Q   Other than monetary rewards, we do not seem to be coming up with many creative ideas. Surely there are some good ideas out there.

A   There definitely are. It would be wise to start with a plan. Decide what you want to accomplish. For example, you probably want to enhance the health of your employees and keep benefits claims down, or you want to keep health up while keeping program costs down. Whatever you want to do, set the reward to target it. However, remember that some secondary reward and aims can also be included. For example, you might want to enhance the overall health of employees with an emphasis on exercise. Offer an incentive and reward to those who walk or jog during lunchtime. If you do it in a way involving the entire company then your secondary reward and aim is also achieved: greater *esprit de corps* or better relationships between the managers and the workers.

Q We like the idea of getting as much bang for our buck on the secondary rewards. What are some other ideas?

A Have a company cookoff in which all employees bring in their favorite dish or cook their favorite recipe. The catch, however, is that the recipe has to be healthy. The winner should be the most healthy and tasty recipe. The CEO can award the annual prize or blue ribbon.

Q We are having trouble coming up with ideas for rewards. That is a problem since my boss is big on this sort of plan. What can we do?

A Organize a committee composed of employees who will receive the reward as well as those who will pay for it: a joint employee-employer one. That way you get the input from both sides for a mutually good project.

Q How do most directors know where to target their rewards?

A A direct way is to assess your claims. Similar to assessing for your company changes, gather all of the claims from the past year, or use another realistic time frame. Examine those claims for amounts and payout, as well as the underlying treatment, disease, or problem. Although this may be difficult, you can probably see themes emerge. For example, a number of employees may have diabetes or hypertension which, while diseases with their own diagnosis, are diseases that also predispose to other complications or illnesses. When these themes emerge, then, target these illnesses or diseases. Education on problems may also be helpful to employees as they may not be aware of the underlying nature of such complications and their contribution or predisposition to other, often more severe, illnesses.

Q What if I do find that heart disease is the underlying problem? Then what? I am not an expert on heart disease.

A No. Nor should you be. However, meet with a physician or a nurse practitioner who is. Think about the underlying issues related to heart disease. The three most important factors are smoking, weight, and exercise. Target those.

Q I would like to reward employees for the additional things that they do, like losing weight or increasing their exercise. However, I am afraid of the risks involved in this sort of behavior modification. What should I do?

A There are two issues here. First, a basic plan that encourages losing weight, increasing exercise, or quitting smoking is a fundamental preventive approach to many diseases. You would, however, encourage all employees in all your written communication to consult with a physician prior to initiating any major change, such as increased exercise.

Q And the heart attack?

A Hopefully, no one will have a heart attack with more exercise. However, untoward events do occur. Again, encourage all employees to have a checkup by a physician prior to any new or changed activity. Be specially attentive to those already overweight, with prior poor health history, and over 40 years of age.

Q I think stress is a big factor in a lot of the problems that I see. I would like to initiate a stress-reduction plan. Could it be a positive influence in our company?

A Many of the strategies mentioned for general good health— healthy diet, daily or scheduled weekly exercise, not smoking, checkups—are also related to stress reduction. See if you can tailor a program that will tie the rewards to stress reduction, putting special attention on exercise. Some exercises are better for reducing stress than others.

Q   We were thinking about a meditation type of program for stress reduction. Is that just too far out for the average company?

A   No, although it might depend on the company, and on the work and product of the company. If you find it enhances the productivity of the company, build it into the health program. On the other hand, you may want a more structured way to introduce meditation, perhaps as a part of a company exercise and relaxation program which is part of a wellness or health promotion plan.

Q   Are there some examples of new approaches using meditation that work?

A   Yes. A recent development is the inclusion of meditation as one of four components in an insured program to reverse heart disease (ONeill 1993, p. A1).

Q   What, in addition to the meditation, is included in this program?

A   The four components are meditation, diet, exercise, and support groups. It will be reimbursed by Mutual of Omaha Insurance Group, and is under consideration for reimbursement by Blue Cross and Blue Shield (O'Neill 1993, p. A1).

Q   We think the heart disease reversal program noted above, and initiated by Dr. Dean Ornish, would be interesting, but aren't there some disadvantages to it?

A   There are clearly skeptics. The major criticism is the ability of participants to be able to remain on the diet and fully implement the program (O'Neill 1993, p. A1). This program would be of interest to benefits administrators as you consider programming for employment.

Q   What are most companies doing in terms of rewards?

A   The majority of companies, according to reports (Piacentini and Foley 1992), are using the deductible amount as an incentive—either decreasing or increasing it contingent upon the employee's behavior—and offering bonuses for healthy behavior.

Q   Are there any legal restrictions on how we can apply incentives?

A   Basically, you need to make sure the categories you develop are defined according to an objective and universal principle. As with discrimination rulings, you would not want to exclude demographic groups of employees. Stay with employees performing at a certain level, or those employees retaining an optimum weight and/or losing so many pounds to attain an optimum weight, which is objective and measurable. That way, each employee has an equal opportunity to participate and you avoid discrimination claims.

Q   My boss wants to reward employees providing positive role models for healthy lifestyles at work. That is a fine ambition, but how would we do it?

A   You might start by defining what you mean by a healthy lifestyle. If you are concerned about bias or values emerging in the definition of lifestyle or just areas that might be excluded from representation, gather a cross-section of your employees into a group and have them work with you. Avoid a subjective definition; use employee input.

Q   If we reward our employees who are more health oriented with a decreased copayment amount, do we also have to decrease the amount of their initial deductible?

A   Not necessarily. You may differentiate between the two, the copayment and deductible, or you could give employees their choice between the two. Before allowing workers to select, analyze the cost differential to be sure choice is what you want.

Q   My CEO thinks it might be a high-level incentive to have a gradual decline in the deductible contribution employees make. It would mean, however, at some point in the future several employees might have next to no deductible. Would this be wise?

A   If the employees earn the various deductible ranges, then removing the potential ceiling or, in this case, the floor on their attainments is an even better incentive. You can have gradations of attainment spanning several years.

Q   What are the things to think about in terms of establishing the categories?

A   The amount of time to attain them as well as the size of each gradation are important. If, for example, the categories are relatively discrete, it would take years to attain the position of no deductible. On the other hand, large jumps might place the employee at the outer range in a few short years. Decide how much of an incentive you want this change in deductible to be and the maximum for employees before implementing the plan.

Q   We plan to survey our 350 employees and see what they prefer in terms of incentives. How does one develop such a questionnaire?

A There are excellent consultants available to assist you in the development of survey questionnaires who may be obtained through educational listings on instrumentation consultation. Another option might be to contact your local college or university and see if any students, perhaps in conjunction with a graduate faculty member, would be willing to take this on for a course project or perhaps as a research project. The latter might be done at minimum cost, if any.

Q Is it true the most popular forms of incentives are still the cash bonuses?

A According to surveys they are (Piacentini and Foley 1992). After legally required benefits and basic retirement and savings, the profit sharing, bonus, and employee stock ownership plans are rated next in percentage of employers offering them.

Q Are there changes predicted in the future for the bonus and profit-sharing plans?

A Perhaps not in the plans themselves, but in terms of pretax dollars, with more cost containment plans. Close behind seem to be pretax offerings that reduce both the overall cost as well as the amount of tax that employees pay. These may be increasingly attractive in the future with parallel increases in taxes.

Q From what I see of our employees, a major incentive would be increased educational leave or support for courses for our employees. Is my perception accurate or not?

A Yes, and it seems to be born out by the statistics from recent studies. Among spending categories by employers, more than 72 percent pay employees for education (Piacentini and Foley 1992). As you might suspect, a larger percentage pay for job-related education than for nonjob-related education.

Q   We think since most of our employees are female, a positive incentive would be to offer child care. Do many firms have child care?

A   Based on data available, only about fiv5 e percent of all companies currently offer child care. However, the numbers are expected to increase; more recent short-term trends reflect an increase among employers offering this benefit. As to the issue of your female workers, you should assume *parents* would find child care desirable (Piacentini and Foley 1992).

Q   For a number of reasons it would be desirable to offer a greater discount on company goods. However, in a recent conversation with our employees, there was not much interest. Since our company would save more on discounts pertaining to our company products, and my boss *is* quite interested in promoting this benefit as an incentive, what should I do?

A   Is there any way it can be linked with health or health promotion? Company goods will not perform as an incentive if employees don't value them. In order for it to work, obviously, the employees need to desire it or the end result. Reassess this one.

Q   We tend to employ a number of blue-collar workers and few white collar. I think we are better off finding incentives that are immediate so the workers can see them. Is this true?

A   I would think so. Employees in general tend to prefer a reward that they can see; that is, one that translates into an immediate reward. Professional employees might prefer a slightly different approach, but this assumption needs to be assessed.

Q We want to be creative and were thinking of offering coupons that could be exchanged for health care benefits. My CEO thinks this program will be too complicated and difficult to manage. I say try it! What do you think?

A While no one would want to squelch creative and innovative ideas, it does sound like it needs to be fully assessed prior to implementation. In a discussion of feasible benefits, one of the disadvantages of such a plan is the time and money required for the initial setup as well as maintenance and administration (Foster 1986).

Q As the director of human resources for a large retail company, I think we already contribute enough to our employees' benefits. I do not think additional incentives are warranted. My CEO disagrees. We offer about $3,000 per employee. Who is right?

A Compared to figures from 1990 on other retail firms, you are above the average amount full-time employees receive in benefits. On average, retail companies contributed a minimum $1,528 annually per employee (Foster 1986).

Q Perhaps we would be better to trade off some of the actual benefits into direct incentives to attain the desired behavioral outcomes of health among our employees that we want. Would this be appropriate?

A While it may be appropriate, you may want to rethink the plan. If you actually take away an evident benefit from employees—even if you trade it back into the package—if employees do not attain it, it is a lost benefit. The result may be a disadvantage for your firm.

Q What would be a better plan?

A Why not leave the benefits package unchanged, then when you do change include incentives in the package. In several years, you will phase in new incentives without directly eroding the apparent outlay of benefits to your workers.

Q Naturally, cash bonuses are good incentives and my boss prefers them. In terms of company savings these are the top-ranked, but several employees prefer health benefits or other nontaxable benefits in contrast to cash bonuses. How can we make this situation work?

A Do these employees fall into certain demographic categories? Are they young or new hires? If you can determine whether they tend to fall into certain categories, it will help you to decide how to proceed from here. It would be natural to find that younger and unmarried employees would not value retirement to the same extent that families or older workers do. Can the workers trade cash for an incentive they do value?

REFERENCES

Business Week. 1993. The new Chrysler. *Business Week Special Edition: The 1993 Business Week 1000. America's Most Valuable Companies*, 49.

Foster, R. 1986. *The Manager's Guide to Employee Benefits*. New York: Facts on File.

O'Neill, M. 1993. Unusual heart therapy wins coverage from big insurers. *New York Times*, 28 July: A1.

Piacentini, J., and Foley, J. 1992. *EBRI Databook on Employee Benefits, 2nd ed.* Washington, D.C.: Employee Benefits Research Institute.

9

Policies, Regulations, and Federal Guidelines

An increasing number of federal and local regulations are dramatically changing the way directors of human resources can manage and enact the benefits for health care of U.S. employees. These regulations, designed to enhance health care benefits for workers, often pose challenges for creating a viable yet cost-effective package for today's, and for tomorrow's, employees. At the same time, there is a need to create a package that also meets the national mandate for cost containment and effectiveness while addressing an escalating number of choices and technologies, all of which add to the costs of implementing benefits. This chapter addresses those challenges with specific regulations and the problems they present for benefits administrators. Problems are categorized in response to the various regulations and their policies, with more emphasis on newer and pending legislation.

LAWS, REGULATIONS, INFORMED CONSENT, AND UNIVERSAL PRECAUTIONS

Q Are there categories of regulations we should be concerned about?

A Yes. Research suggests there are four main categories of laws that mandate benefits (EBRI 1987). These are: kind of services covered, providers or those who qualify to perform and be reimbursed for benefits covered, continuation or conversion addressing the length of time for coverage, and dependents or who is covered under a particular coverage package.

Q Are there recent bills and regulations I should worry about pertaining to disabilities?

A The most sweeping and also the most recent is the Americans with Disabilities Act of 1990. It is linked with prior ERISA laws, but outlines regulations of its own.

Q What is informed consent?

A *Informed consent* emerged during the recent decades of increasing research and concerns for the rights of research subjects, who often are patients. Informed consent means that an investigator who engages in research or in experimental treatments of patients which bear on research, must provide the subject with enough information to make a well-informed decision. Information regarding the risks, benefits, or payment, for example, involved in such procedures must be fully revealed.

Q Are there legal implications of informed consent?

A Absolutely! If an individual is not provided with information, is provided with inaccurate information, or is deceived about a procedure, especially in cases where federal funding is involved by hospitals providing Medicare reimbursement, funding can be withheld. Violation of informed consent is a serious offense.

Q What are universal precautions?

A Universal precautions refer to the use of a standard set of medical or medically related procedures universally implemented to minimize risk when one might be exposed to contagious diseases. Acquired Immune Deficiency Syndrome (AIDS) is just one example of the diseases for which universal precautions should be used.

Q Are there varying degrees, or levels, of universal precautions?

A Yes. The level is contingent upon the degree of risk assumed for the particular treatment, disease, or between the parties involved.

Q What is minimum universal precaution?

A The use of a mask and gloves is minimum. A dentist will, today, almost always use a mask and gloves in general treatment with all patients.

Q What, then, is the maximum level of universal precaution?

A When risk is assessed to be especially high, for example, when there is known presence of infection, risk is assessed to be high, especially in light of probable exposure to body fluids or blood. In those instances the maximum of precaution is implemented: Protective items are usually provided by the institution, such as a hospital.

Q Why is it called universal?

A The term *universal* means that these are standard precautions, not particular to one individual, but a set of precautions universally applied by health care providers.

Q I know the American Drug Association (ADA) regulations are changing in today's health care climate. Where can I find out about them?

A There are several standard sources of information that will provide you information on regulations. It is essential to a human resource director to have up-to-date information both on the rules and regulations as well as their implications.

Q Since we are a small company, would it be better to drop all coverage for drastic or long-term illnesses?

A Costwise, it might be, although I know employers who are reluctant to take such a drastic step with loyal employees. However, since the costs are enormous and cannot be shared across large numbers of employees in smaller firms, there is a tendency for smaller companies to drop this coverage altogether. To avoid discrimination problems make sure the coverage is fair by treating all employees the same.

Q Can we drop claims for catastrophic medical costs for treatments like transplant surgery?

A Yes and no. You can if you drop coverage for all participants in a similar way for all employees. You cannot, however, if you discriminate and specify a particular illness.

Q What is to keep us from specifying a particular illness?

A The provisions under the Americans with Disabilities Act prohibit the specification of a particular illness. You are not required, however, to offer coverage as an employer as long as you treat all employees the same.

CHALLENGES OF SPECIFIC ILLNESSES

Q One of my employees has just been diagnosed with AIDS. What should I tell my boss?

A Nothing. According to federal guidelines and the current acceptance of confidentiality, information which you receive in the service of your position as the human resource director cannot be disclosed to other employees, even one's boss. However, if you have the employee's permission it is a different situation. Tread carefully.

Q Shouldn't my boss know when several of the employees in our company develop symptoms of an illness?

A Follow current guidelines, of course, which stress the importance of confidentiality. However, it would not be inappropriate to indicate employee claims have the potential of increasing, or are increasing, in certain areas.

Q A man about 40 years of age in our company is showing signs of rather severe illness. He really does look terrible and other employees have noticed. So far, his work is going well but I wonder if I shouldn't talk to him. He came in the other day and was asking about his benefits. He is very concerned because he knows we will be cutting back shortly. What should I do?

A You cannot inquire directly. However, you could allude to your concern, comment that he seems preoccupied and worried about his benefits, and ask if there is any particular concern he has. Express your own concern. Nevertheless, unless he discloses any specific information to you, you will need to leave the door open and wait.

Q What can I tell my other employees about a colleague who has just been diagnosed with AIDS? They are genuinely concerned about him.

A It is wonderful that your company's fellow employees are concerned about a coworker and they should be encouraged to share their concerns directly with him. However, you cannot divulge information about any employee to another employee in the work force. Confidentiality is a guideline of benefits coverage among companies.

Q An employee came into my office and complained a co-worker has been absent a lot lately. She is angry because he seems to be slacking off at work and has taken a lot of illness time. She wants to know what is going on. I am aware this employee has been diagnosed with an HIV infection and understand her concerns. I, too, am concerned with the employee and the company productivity. But, what can I tell her?

A You may tell her you are aware of her concern; you, too, are concerned with the company's productivity. You may add you are also aware that employees have rights regarding privacy. You may also comment on the obvious: Her fellow employee has been ill, but you are not free to discuss any illness or its nature with other employees. Encourage her to return to work and assure her that if she were in a similar situation, you as the human resource director would look out for her concerns and privacy. Close by expressing your appreciation for her concern.

Q We are a relatively small company with less than 50 employees. Will size make a difference in covering drastic illnesses such as cancer?

A Yes, it will. For the smaller company, those usually under 50 employees, the costs are more difficult to spread over the smaller numbers of employees. Thus, it becomes a much more costly endeavor to cover such drastic illnesses or claims.

Q What can I tell some of my employees about their concerns about contracting AIDS or hepatitis B? Several workers have wondered if our firm will begin to cover more long-term and catastrophic illnesses. Two parents with young children have been in to talk with me three times; they think they may get it from an employee whom they suspect of having the virus.

A It sounds as if your firm needs an in-service meeting regarding the transmission of the viruses with time for a question and answer session. As part of the health benefits program, this would be an appropriate and proactive move. Combine it with any offering under your health promotion programming. There are, of course, other diseases one would be concerned with as well. Keep the information both specific but inclusive and broad to avoid a focus only on AIDS or hepatitis and their related complications.

EMPLOYEES WITH CHALLENGES: DISABILITIES

Q Can I drop coverage for a disabled employee?

A Not unless you drop coverage for all employees. Under the discrimination clause in the Act for Americans with Disabilities, you need to provide the same coverage for all employees (McKee 1993, p. 20). Or, you must drop the same coverage for all employees. Avoid categories of coverage that restrict coverage in certain illnesses or diseases.

Q We are a self-insured company and do not purchase outside insurance. Do the disabilities acts apply to us?

A Yes. According to recent court rulings the act applies equally to self-insured as well as companies purchasing some insurance through another party or company.

Q As the director of human resources in our small company, I am confused about the new regulations and policies on disabilities. What are the key features?

A You are not the only one who is confused. However, the key features for a person in your position are the following: Section 1630.4 on employment states an employer cannot discriminate on the basis of disability pertaining to hiring and recruitment, pay rates, assignments of tasks, leaves of absence, and fringe benefits offered as part of the employment. These mandates went into effect in 1990 (McKee 1993, p. 21).

Q Aren't there some disability regulations allowing a company to assess for risk? What are they and how do they work?

A The section on insurance, Section 36.212, does state that an insurer can "classify risks," however, this section is, in some ways, a contradiction of an earlier section on discrimination (McKee 1993, p. 22). Make sure you document well to cover you and your company.

Q Is there a central location to get ongoing information on the new Americans with Disabilities Act?

A   Yes. The federal government has a hot line. The number is 1-800-949-4232.

Q   In our state it is very difficult to classify on the basis of risk for health insurance. However, we have ended up with a number of high-risk employees and I would like to put them into a separate category. Is it true I can do that?

A   It is true under the disabilities act you may classify on the basis of risk. It specifically states directors may use "risk classification" and underwriting policies as long as they are legal in your company's state (Piacentini and Foley 1992). Check carefully.

Q   We do not want to be caught in a discrimination suit. Is it true, however, that those workers with a disability get a longer period of continued coverage under the recent Consumer Omnibus Budget Reconciliation Act (COBRA)* changes?

A   Yes. The time period for continuation has changed; there is a longer time period for optional purchase of continued coverage for disabled workers if they are disabled at the time employment is terminated (Piacentini and Foley 1992). The time is 36 months.

Q   What advice do you have as to what an administrator for benefits could say to a disabled employee who will terminate soon. The young woman has been disabled since birth, she is not working well here, and will seek other employment. However, she also wants to purchase our health coverage under the changed COBRA regulations. When I

---

*Among other stipulations COBRA provides for continued health care coverage for terminated employees.

told her it would also have a limited coverage time, she was quite disturbed. What can I do?

A   You might point out to her this is a longer time period than other employees receive, and it will be longer if she is a dependent of a former employee. There is, essentially, nothing else you can do without risking incurring discrimination claims from other employees.

Q   We have had only a few disabled employees in the past, although those we have had were great workers. One disabled man who is leaving for other reasons wants extended coverage. However, he does not want to pay a different premium for the extra extended coverage time. Do I have the option of not raising the premium?

A   Yes. You may retain a lower limit, but then you would need to do so for all employees. This does set a precedent (Piacentini and Foley 1992).

FAMILY LEAVE BILL

Q   What are the key features of the family leave law? I have an employee who is prone to litigation, and I want to prevent problems in regulations when I can.

A   This is a smart and proactive stance. The key features of this law, which went into effect in August of 1993, are the following: It applies to companies with 50 or more employees; it provides up to 12 unpaid leave weeks per year; and the employees need to have been employed by the company for 12 or more months and for more than 1,250 hours. The stipulations apply for a child, spouse, parent, or worker (self) needing care. Employers must guarantee their workers that they will return to similar and equivalent jobs and continue the preleave benefits. On the other hand, if the employee does not return to work, the employer may recover the health care benefits premiums paid.

Q   What is the most important dimension of the new family leave benefit regulations for us?

A   Documentation (Maynard 1993, p. 26). Keep records of all exchanges and include a worker signature to verify you discussed it with the employee.

Q   In terms of the new family leave law, do I have any rights as an employer? It seems to me that all the emphasis is on the worker.

A   There are stipulations for both parties. Employers may require an employee who is on the family leave to verify continuing status and intention of returning to work (Maynard 1993, p. 26). In addition, using salary as a calculation, it is possible to remove the top 10 percent of the work force from the leave based on their pay. The highest remunerated employees would be exempt.

Q   Aren't there some federal regulations and guidelines we can use? Are they available?

A   The family leave went into effect prior to the enactment of the federal guidelines (Maynard 1993, p. 26). They were a high priority and were to be developed by June 1993. The Labor Department developed the guidelines for the Family Leave Bill.

Q   We are working on the new family leave as part of our benefits package. We find this adds greatly to our costs. Is this true of other companies?

A   Much of this answer depends on the proportion you have in females of childbearing age, for example. However, looking nationally, in the late 1980s the Chamber of Commerce estimated $2.6 billion would be used to replace those employees on family leave (EBRI 1987). This estimate included payments for continuing health benefits and the reimbursement to a replacement worker.

Q   Having been in the administration of benefits for a long time, one develops a certain ability to assess employees. Today an employee who wants a family leave came in with a medical certification. I think it is a fraudulent document. Is it all right to check up on her?

A   Careful. According to the Labor Department, employers cannot "pursue" an employee even when suspecting fraud (Nobel 1993, p. F23).

Q   Is there nothing I can do in the case of a questionable certification?

A   Yes. While you cannot pursue the employee, you may request—and perhaps pay for—additional medical opinions. Request a second and even a third opinion (Nobel 1993, p. F23). Suggest a reputable physician you can trust as one of the two or three.

Q   An employee tells me she must take a family leave to care for her ailing father. This is the first time that her coworkers or I have heard about an ailing father, or a father at all. May I check to see what the situation is without breaching the Family Leave Bill?

A   Unfortunately for employers, you may not. Details about the medical situation that initiates the leave request cannot be obtained by an employer from employees regarding the family situation (Nobel 1993, p. F23). Grant the leave.

Q   Family leaves are creating problems for us. Last year a valued employee took a family leave of 12 weeks, and now he wants to add the 12 weeks from this year on to it. In essence, he will have 24 weeks of family leave strung together. Is this legal under the Family Leave Bill?

A   It is legal, however cumbersome it might be for both the benefits administrator and the company's supervisor (Nobel 1993, p. F23). The bill allows such combinations.

RETIREMENT REGULATIONS

Q   Is it true the private insurance for the elderly is declining?

A   Yes. In the past ten years the coverage by private insurance of the elderly has declined by a few percentage points and continues to decline (Piacentini and Foley 1992, p. 226).

Q   Since the laws are changing on retirement packages, we thought maybe we should move into more VEBA accounts. Would it be feasible, especially if we drop the retirement benefits?

A   Voluntary Employees' Beneficiary Associations (VEBAs) are taxable, thus your company might want to consider the Voluntary Retirement Health Plans (VRHPs) introduced in 1987, which are tax deductible for the employee. The VEBAs were enacted as part of the Deficit Reduction Act of 1984. In contrast, VRHPs encourage employers to address health and long-term benefits of retirees and the interest is not subject to federal taxes (EBRI 1987). Assess each carefully.

Q We are having discussions about the relatively new retirement equity. What is the focus?

A Under the Retirement Equity Act (REA) enacted in 1984, the aim was to ". . . promote economic equity for women" (**EBRI** 1987).

Q What is the key provision in the REA?

A The main aim is removal of penalties against women entering the work force at ". . . young ages and then having children" (**EBRI** 1987).

Q What are provisions we need to be concerned with in terms of retirement benefits?

A There are three. Workers may leave and return to jobs without penalty in a set time period without losing pension credits, benefits plans for pensions cannot claim as a break a leave for maternity/paternity reasons, and the minimum age for enrollment in private pension plans and for vesting is lower (**EBRI** 1987).

Q Are there other features which would affect employees?

A Yes. Among other features would be granting widows and widowers the death benefits for a spouse's pension if the pension is vested, and recognition of a homemaker's contribution in calculating pensions (**EBRI** 1987).

Q Are these laws part of a larger bill?

A Yes. The **REA** is a part of the larger benefits package passed by Congress to address the overall economic equity of women, called the Economic Equity Act (EEA) (**EBRI** 1987).

Q We have fewer than 20 participants in our simplified employee plan (SEP). Can our company take deferrals for pensions?

A Yes. Since your company does not have more than 25 participants you may defer, but the maximum limit is $7,000. However, the other criterion is that half of the participants elect to make contributions (EBRI 1987).

Q When did changes in the SEPs occur?

A This change occurred as part of the Tax Reform Act of 1986, in which employees may also contribute pretax dollars to accounts (EBRI 1987).

Q One of my employees wants to retire soon and she is confused by all the retirement mandates. Can she simplify her situation and allow us to consolidate into one package?

A Yes. Consolidation is one purpose of the Simplified Employee Pension (SEP). Workers can consolidate monies from different sources through one SEP (EBRI 1987).

Q Would it be accurate if I told an employee who is about to retire that the laws on the SEPs are similar to IRAs she already has? This might help her feel less confused.

A Yes. An IRA would be a useful analogy. The SEP laws are similar, but not exactly the same as those of the IRAs in terms of asset transfers or restrictions (EBRI 1987).

Q We think it would be wise to try to limit our retirement package costs by specifying certain categories of retirees. Several of these employees who are more costly want to purchase term life insurance. Can we do that?

A   Probably not. Check, but under the Tax Reform Act of 1984, discrimination is ruled out for retirees' term life insurance (Piacentini and Foley 1992), among several other features of the tax reform.

Q   At the same time, we have 15 employees—out of 150—who will retire in the next decade. They seem particularly interested in the ability to use their annuities from one of two universal life insurance plans we have. Can they do this? How should I advise them?

A   They may withdraw early under certain qualifying provisions. One of them is the tax penalty on early withdrawal of annuities from universal life insurance introduced with the 1984 Tax Reform Act (Piacentini and Foley 1992). Advise them to balance the need for early withdrawal with the tax loss on the overall annuity. They may lose more than they gain.

Q   Although we continue to use a modified cafeteria plan, the new rules make it less attractive for retirement to our executive employees. Two of our executives want the majority of their benefits in the cafeteria plan. This may put them up to about 45 percent in benefits which are nontaxable. Is this OK to do?

A   From what you say, it sounds as if the employees will have too large a proportion of their benefits in nontaxable benefits within the parameters set for cafeteria plans. If these employees elect this plan and proportion, then they need to be aware of the full implications of these changes. The 1984 Deficit Reduction Act regulated the benefits plans for cafeteria types. For example, if employees receive more than 25 percent of their benefits in nontaxable benefits, the available taxable benefits may be taxed for certain employees. The total amount needs to be calculated against this regulation, especially as a liability for retirement.

Q   We have several employees who are in high salary categories. There is a "ceiling" on the salary ranges. These employees want to return to school and receive MBAs. Since we have an employee educational benefits program, can they use educational benefits and not pay taxes on the educational package?

A   No. If they are in the highly remunerated salary range their benefits for education may be taxed. This information needs to be conveyed to the employees as a part of the annual benefits communication, especially since the tax is usually paid up front. It may be recovered either in part or fully. If employees are retired it may pose a burden on their set funds, since taxes may be paid prior to calculations.

Q   Our company has been on shaky ground for the past two fiscal years. I have been under the gun to cut back as much as possible. What about our retirees who are responsible for a hefty amount in health care bills? Can we cut them out if we file for bankruptcy?

A   No. If they are currently covered under the retirement health benefits plan, according to the changes instituted in 1988, your company needs to plan to continue with payments for health and life insurance benefits (Piacentini and Foley 1992).

Q   What if we need to modify our plan in order to avoid going bankrupt?

A   Under specific circumstances, one of which is bankruptcy, the law allows alterations to avoid liquidation (Piacentini and Foley 1992). Your firm will need to provide proof of need to make changes in retirees' benefits.

COBRA LAWS AND CONTINUED COVERAGE

Q Since we are a small company, with only 21 employees, is it true that we do not need to plan on offering the employees our company is laying off any health care?

A No. Not unless employees leave of their own accord prior to layoffs. The Consolidated Omnibus Budget Reconciliation Act (often known as the COBRA law), passed in 1985, states any company with 20 or more employees must offer departing employees the option of continued coverage through purchase for 18 months, 29 months for the disabled, or employees' dependents covered up to 36 months (for example, divorced or widowed). Given the number of employees in your company, you come under the COBRA Law.

Q We are interested in what we should do under the COBRA law. In our state, the COBRA federal stipulation extends longer than our company's. We only have employees in one state. What must we do?

A According to the laws, state regulations will be superseded by federal mandates for the COBRA law. Thus, you will need to abide by the federal law in this case. Where there is a difference, the federal stipulation takes precedent.

Q Do we have to add our state continuation length for the COBRA law to the federal length? In other words, do we need to total our state and federal length?

A Not at this time. The federal takes precedent but you are not required to add the state continuation amount (EBRI 1987).

Q Last week we terminated an employee due to poor conduct on the job; he had been with us for five years. At the time he was angry but knew it was inevitable. Now, he would like to continue to purchase his health insurance with us. Do I have to allow this option?

A   No. In most instances the employee who leaves has the right to continued coverage. One primary exclusion is the employee who is terminated for poor performance or misconduct (Piacentini and Foley 1992).

Q   We do not understand the breadth of the COBRA law. Can we exclude self-insurance since we are a small company?

A   No. There are no exceptions made in the COBRA law. All health benefits are addressed by this law (EBRI 1987).

Q   An employee told me that her husband has asked her for a divorce; she is worried about her health benefits which are through his company. She wants to know if she should purchase our benefits plan. However, we just raised our deductible and it is quite high for her salary range. How should I advise her?

A   Give her a week or two to pull together and, as part of assessing her situation, give her an assignment. Have her collect information on the actual cost for your plan and for that of her husband's company, including the possibility of continued purchase. She may continue to purchase coverage with his company up to 36 months following the divorce. Compare these costs using equivalent benefits coverage; see which is less expensive, taking into consideration the time limit on the other company. Also, if the other company's is less expensive at the start, would it be feasible to purchase your firm's at the end of the 36 months? She will then know which decision is best. Can the continued coverage be a part of the negotiated divorce agreement?

Advise her to consult a lawyer, especially if she has been married for ten years or more.

OTHER PROBLEMS

Q What is the new act on managed care which passed in 1993?

A The American Health Security Act (AHS) of 1993. The purpose is to replace and strengthen the 1992 bill regarding single-payer alternatives to managed competition proposals (*Health Policy Advisory Center Bulletin* 1993, p. 43).

Q Who introduced the American Health Security Act of 1993?

A S-491, HR 1200, was the development of Senator Paul Wellstone (D-MN), Representative John Conyers (D-MN), and Representative Jim McDermott (D-WA), plus numerous cosponsors (*Health Policy Advisory Center Bulletin* 1993, p. 43).

Q What are the key features of the AHS Act?

A Essentially, all legal U.S. residents would have health insurance under a program called the American Health Security Program. A card certifying entitlement for the stated benefits is expected to be implemented.

Q How do they affect us in benefits?

A If the entire program passes, it could replace some benefits currently offered by employers or it may be that employers could purchase these as employee benefits. Within this bill, obviously, would be a greater emphasis on the managed-care services such as health maintenance organizations. If used by employers, these would reduce overall benefits costs. Until the full plan evolves the total ramifications will not be clear.

Q   What is the critical difference in the way in which it may affect benefits?

A   The security health bill, which differs from many proposals for managed-competition or managed-care approaches, bases eligibility for services received on ". . . residency rather than on place of employment" (*Health Policy Advisory Center Bulletin* 1993, p. 43). This feature of the bill would be a critical difference between future and past programs, especially for benefits programming.

Q   Is it true that we will be required to have a utilization review on all of our claims before they will be paid?

A   Not unless you have review stated in your contract. It is true, however, that an increasing number of treatments are under scrutiny, including certain types of surgery.

Q   Is it true that, under Title VII, we cannot offer benefits that take gender into account?

A   According to Title VII employers cannot discriminate on a number of features including sex (Harrington 1985). Differential rates cannot be set.

Q   There seem to be a number of regulations recently paying more and more attention to the low wage earner and the uninsured. Why is this?

A   The complete answer to that question would be lengthy. However, in brief, the uninsured also cost employers by raising the overall medical costs passed on to companies as evidenced in rising insurance rates. Since, historically, the majority of insured obtain insurance from their employers this affects business nationally. It is a complex phenomenon.

Q In terms of our communication, what do we have to communicate to our employees? We would prefer to use more e-mail and less paper. Is this OK?

A Maybe, but you do need records and the e-mail may not meet this criterion. According to regulations there are three things you must communicate to your employees. They are the summary annual report (SAR), the benefits statement, and the summary plan description (SPD) (Foster 1986). These are the minimum and you need a written record to verify that you conveyed this information in writing to all employees.

COMMUNICATING WITH EMPLOYEES

Q Are there other reasons why electronic forms of communication may not work or meet federal or state regulations?

A Absolutely. Many employees do not find computers user friendly. It also might be impossible for an employee to convey the information to a family member at home or to take it home to read and study. Although times are changing, electronic communication may not meet standards as written communication.

Q Is there a trend toward more use of computers and less paper communication?

A Yes. However for your purposes in benefits administration, also make sure you have a written record, not just a computer transaction. Get and keep a hard copy.

Q We have several older employees who are concerned because we do not send them annual SPD reports. Do we need to do so more than once every five years?

A The law states a minimum of every five years in the event of plan changes, and ten years without benefit changes (Foster 1986). Explain this regulation to your employees.

Q What are some other creative ways we can convey the information we need to, while making it more attractive, interesting, and easily read?

A Here is a quick list of several possibilities which you will need to assess in terms of time spent in preparation, number of employees in the company, and the type of industry and employee you have. Try these for a start: looseleaf inserts, specialized publications, internal publications, membership cards, or individual benefits statements and summaries, in addition to the usual memos or letters (Foster 1986).

Q What regulations set the tone for the amount of communication we are required to do?

A Most—but not all—of these mandates harken back to the ERISA law of 1974 (Foster 1986).

Q How successful is it to use nontraditional means of communicating with employees? For instance, do other companies use computers, presentations, and such?

A Yes. Presentations are an excellent means of conveying new information to a group, such as a new group of recruits, new personnel at a hospital, or a new trainee group. With the introduction of computers quality overheads and slides can be readily made for an interesting presentation.

Q   We are a company with more than 35 employees and we are using an HMO. Is it true that we need to offer a dual option in a federally qualified HMO if one requests it?

A   No. Companies no longer are required to offer this option for dual enrollment in a federally qualified HMO at their (the HMO's) request. This regulation which was in effect until 1988, is eliminated in the Health Maintenance Organization Act Amendment.

Q   What was the objective of the HMO amendment?

A   The key is more flexibility in the negotiations that employers utilize for coverage and rates. Essentially, the aim was cost reduction for benefits packages among HMOs (Piacentini and Foley 1992).

REFERENCES

The American Health Security Act of 1993. 1993. *Health Policy Advisory Center Bulletin* 23(1), Spring: 43.

Employee Benefits Research Institute (EBRI). 1987. *Government Mandating of Employee Benefits.* Washington, D.C.: EBRI.

Foster, R. 1986. *The Manager's Guide to Employee Benefits.* New York: Facts on File.

Harrington, G. 1985. *The Health Insurance Fact & Answer Book.* New York: Harper & Row.

Maynard, R. 1993. Meet the new law on family leave. *Nation's Business,* April: 26.

McKee, B. 1993. The disabilities labyrinth. *Nation's Business,* April: 18–25.

Nobel, B. 1993. Interpreting the Family Leave Act. *New York Times,* 1 August: F23.

Piacentini, J., and Foley, J. 1992. *EBRI Databook on Employee Benefits, 2nd ed.* Washington, D.C.: EBRI.

10

Part-Time and Temporary Employees

Employment on a part-time basis is becoming increasingly important to employers in an era of cost containment. Likewise, the use of temporary workers, or temps, is also on the increase. One challenging dimension of part-time and temporary employment is the benefits package for these workers. The range of solutions to this problem is as varied as the questions. This chapter explores a number of key problems that involve part-time and temporary employees. In particular, it explores the possibility of not offering benefits, and the resulting problems as well as modifications in the current part-time package. Options being examined by other companies are also discussed as examples to guide the proactive human resource director.

PART-TIME EMPLOYEES

Q Just what are the facts on part-time employment in the U.S.?

A According to surveys, in 1991 there were 2,302,000 part-time employees (Scott 1993). Recent news reports state part-time employment is quite high and continuing to expand faster than other segments of the employment puzzle.

Q   Are the numbers among part-time workers on the increase?

A   Absolutely. It is predicted that by the turn of the century part-timers may make up more than half of the American work force (Piacentini and Foley 1992).

Q   Does this trend of increasing numbers of part-time workers primarily involve women or is it also increasing among men?

A   While the number of women working part-time is increasing at a more rapid rate than for men, the number of male part-time workers is also increasing.

Q   Are most companies offering health care benefits to their part-time employees?

A   This varies widely. The current trend is to reduce benefits, especially for the part-timer. In most instances, part-time employees are hit with the major portion of the cuts, if not losing benefits altogether.

Q   We would like to eliminate benefits for health care for all of our part-time employees as a cost-cutting feature. Is this worth the hassle?

A   It depends on three key questions only you can answer. The questions are: how many part-time employees do you have, how invested are you in them, and, more important, how essential are they to your organization? Once you have clear answers to these questions you have the information on which to make a good decision.

Q Financially, it would be better if we did not offer any benefits to our part-time employees. Does this seem unfair?

A Many companies do not offer benefits to part-time employees, which is why part-timers are so attractive to employers. Go back and take a look at what you have been offering in contrast to what your final objective is. If not offering any benefits to part-timers represents a major alteration, then keep the final outcome the same, that is, no offer of benefits. However, you will need to change your strategy to implement this change.

Q This issue of what is defined as part-time is getting more complicated every day. We have always used the 20-hour workweek as a marker for part-time employment. However, I have an employee who works part-time and she says she is not truly part-time because she works more than half of the current average workweek. Based on this argument she wants health care benefits. Is she right?

A Let's start with the fact that in 1990 the American work schedule for non-farm-related work averaged 39 hours per week (Piacentini and Foley 1992, pp. 465–68). However, most firms use the 20-hour work week as a definition of part-time, although you may define it as less, or half of 39.

Q For the sake of calculating benefits, what was the average part-time worker working in hours per week in recent surveys?

A In 1990, the part-timer worked an average across all types of work of 20.2 hours per week (Piacentini and Foley 1992, pp. 465–68). Most employers use the 20-hour figure as the marker for calculation of benefits.

Q   Where are the largest numbers of part-time workers located?

A   The service industries hire the largest proportion of part-timers (Piacentini and Foley 1992, pp. 465–68).

Q   What is the proportion among service employees who work part-time?

A   Thirty-six percent of all employees in occupations that are defined as service work part-time. This is compared to all workers in the U.S. where the proportion is around 18 percent (Piacentini and Foley 1992, pp. 465–68).

Q   We are thinking of reducing the administrative levels between the associates to the CEO and the direct line supervisors. However, a number of these administrative employees are also part-time. Thus, if we eliminate them, it may cut costs overall but it will reflect in a proportionate increase in the benefits outlay. How do I avoid having benefits be held responsible for increasing costs?

A   While organizations are being flattened, the greatest proportion of part-timers are not among administrative personnel, who do, however, have the shortest overall work-week at 40.5 hours per week on average (Piacentini and Foley 1992, pp. 465–68).

Q   My boss called me in to discuss changes in our overall work force because he wants more productive workers with a bit more experience. He is also interested in additional ways to cut costs in our benefits. However, if we move to hiring more middle-aged employees I think we lose the proportion of those who work part-time and receive no benefits. I think this whole thing may backfire. What do you think?

A   It is possible. When one examines the data on age related to working part-time, the younger worker is more likely to seek part-time employment—about 90 percent in the category between 16 and 24 years of age (Piacentini and Foley 1992, pp. 465–68).

Q   Where are the big jumps in part-time workers?

A   After age 24, the number of part-timers drops considerably—to about 13 percent—until workers reach retirement age (Piacentini and Foley 1992, pp. 456–68).

Q   We have a new company opening in a different region in which I have to set up the health benefits program. My mandate is to get as many good employees without benefits as is possible. I know from my 12 years administering benefits, women work more often in part-time positions than men. Can we just hire more women and not offer any benefits?

A   You may hire only if you follow the nondiscrimination laws, even though you are correct that women work part-time in a larger proportion than do men.

Q   We want to compare our part-time workers and some possible benefits with other categories of workers. Among all workers and the various types of industries, where are the part-timers?

A   Data are usually categorized into four occupational types whether full- or part-time: Managerial has 11 percent; technical and sales has 21 percent; services has 36 percent; and production has a little more than 8 percent part-time workers (Piacentini and Foley 1992, pp. 465–68).

Q   A valued part-time employee who has been with our company for a long time in terms of part-timers, stopped me in the cafeteria. She made an appointment to talk with me about getting some health care benefits now that she has turned 50 years old. She said: ". . . a lot of part-timers have health care insurance." I did not think this was the situation. Is she correct?

A   It depends on what you read. The overall national trend is away from health care benefits for part-timers. However, a study last year on the numbers of American workers who were uninsured reported that among part-time employees, only 15 percent were uninsured (EBRI 1987). What is missing from this report, however, is the information on the source of the health care insurance. The report did not specify whether employers provided the insurance; it is only reported a certain percentage is uninsured or insured.

Q   Is it possible some of those part-time and insured employees are not insured by their employer?

A   Of course. It is highly possible, for example, since the majority of part-timers are female, that they are covered by a spouse's plan.

Q   Are we going to be pressed into health care benefits for the part-timers as well? I see statistics that suggest this may be the case by the next decade.

A   The aim of health care reform will be health care access, with coverage for all workers. This includes full- and part-time workers.

Q   If our company wants to retain some benefits for our part-time employees, what is the best approach?

A   The part-time employees can be assessed in terms of a proportion or a relative weight in comparison to the benefits of the full-time employees. What would seem especially appropriate in today's climate is a portion of what the full-time employees receive.

Q   What about an approach to moving in the direction of part-time reductions?

A   The same approach used for full-time employees can also be used with the part-time employees. The most acceptable for the employee is a phase-in approach.

Q   How would one go about a phase-in?

A   Adequate announcement and planning time is needed for both the company as well as the employee. While most employees know changes are pending, they do need to face the reality of the actual change. Most employees, or anyone for that matter, do not address and implement a change until it is imminent. Therefore, announce the actual change and give employees time to make alternative plans. The suggested minimum time frame for these changes is about three months. However, time will depend on the degree and nature of the cuts. Allow longer time if you plan to eliminate all benefits in health care for part-time employees who have previously had that benefit.

Q   What if our part-time employees threaten to leave if the company eliminates their whole health care benefits package?

A   This is a threat or a chance that your company should anticipate and think through, very thoroughly, prior to announcing such a change. It would be a major tactical mistake to announce and then withdraw, especially if you anticipate other changes down the road.

Q   How can I decide if it is worth keeping part-time benefits or not?

A   To some extent this is a subjective assessment. However, you can be more objective by assessing the contributions and productivity of your part-time employees, and adding to that the overall assessment of what company productivity would be if you did not have them. What are their essential contributions? What do you save by having part-time employees? If their contributions, in contrast to the company outlays, are minimum, then you have the answer.

Q   Some of our part-time employees view themselves as essential to our company and are quite loyal to the business. Can I differentiate among part-timers with benefits?

A   You cannot differentiate among part-timers' benefits without also running the danger of being caught in a discrimination case. You need a plan, a policy as it were, so part-time employees are treated in a nondiscriminatory and just manner. If, for instance, you have a similar policy for a level of benefit corresponding to a level in the company, you could offer the same benefit to both full- and part-time employees. Or, you might want to offer the same benefit in a slightly graduated and less complete package to the part-time employee to differentiate from the full-time employee. But, if, as you suggest, some of your part-timers are as solid and loyal as full-time employees, perhaps a similar offering is more in line with the message and commitment you want to convey.

Q   Our company prides itself on our image in the community as a company that cares. We have a number of part-time employees who live in this community. My boss is concerned if we cut part-time benefits to save money, we may alienate the community. We need to sell our products in this community as well as in other communities. What would you suggest to solve this problem?

A   You need to do some prior proactive work before you announce and implement any cuts. A clear message of the value of the part-timers and the importance of their contribution is needed here. An announcement including cuts for all employees may be your best approach. Then, implement them.

Q   We are concerned that in our company, which is medium-sized and product-oriented, we will end up with tensions between part-time and full-time employees. At this time we have about 30 percent part-time employees. Any suggestions?

A   There must be some reason you suspect intergroup tensions. What is going on now which you can address to diffuse potential problems? It is always wise to solve minor disputes before they erupt into major ones, if you can. With this in mind assess the current issues: Are they inherent in the situation, are they related to health care benefits, or is there some other problem you need to address first? If there is, tend to it before this problem becomes worse.

Q   We pride ourselves on being a company that treats all employees fairly and in a similar manner. This includes our part-time employees. Now my boss tells me to cut benefits for health care of all of our part-time employees. She says this is the current trend. Is she right?

A   Yes and no. It is accurate according to surveys that part-time benefits are eroding as many companies move to no part-time health care. However, you need to assess your particular company and where it is in light of your image and the need you have for part-time employees. Do you know what this change will do to your part-time work force; how essential are they to the company?

Q I do not see much information about retaining part-time employees and their benefits. Is this an obsolete idea, using part-timers and providing them benefits?

A No. But it is an area under strong scrutiny. Given recent cutbacks and cost containment, it is an easy target for downsizing of the overall benefits plan. You need to assess such a move in light of your individual company needs, your employees—both full- and part-time—and the need for parity among the two groups.

Q We understand one of the aims of health reform is something called "health security." Does security imply we need to provide health benefits coverage for our part-time employees which we currently do not provide?

A The answer is unclear. However, the reform aim of securing health for all employees does suggest that all employees, part- and full-time, would be included but perhaps proportionally based on amount of work.

Q We are thinking of combining our worker compensation and our health insurance programming under one office, but we do not want to create an unmanageable problem. What are the advantages?

A You may end up saving money, because few companies coordinate these two programs. However, if it occurs, an advantage of combining is being able to compare the claims for the same situation filed under both offices, a form of "double dipping" (*Nation's Business*, p. 33).

Q   Is it true that the part-timer is less motivated than the full-time employee? And, if it is the case, would it work to use health care benefits to improve on motivation?

A   Data do not substantiate the assumption that part-timers are less motivated. However, if you want to motivate an employee, health care benefits are a valued reward in today's market.

Q   We are troubled by an image in our community as a company that uses a lot of part-time employees. Also, there is a community sense they are "exploited" since part-timers do not receive any benefits. Is this image typical?

A   It all depends on what you negotiate, although this is an increasingly common and troublesome image among firms. If your employees know from the outset that they will not have benefits, they can negotiate accordingly.

Q   We do not offer benefits to our part-time employees. Will we need to offer a higher salary or hourly wage to them?

A   Wages would depend on the market in your environment and on the hourly wage you currently use. It would not, however, be a bad idea in terms of company relations with part-timers.

Q   If we offer a higher wage to our part-timers because they do not get benefits we may alienate some of our full-time employees. What do other companies do about this?

A   The problem of intergroup tensions between part- and full-time employees is historical. However, given the radical shifts in hiring, turnover, and employer–employee relations, you may find it an advantage. The rationale for a high wage is clear: It replaces a desirable benefit.

Q   We are using many more part-time employees than in the past—several of them are really fine workers. I suggested to our CEO we offer health care benefits as an incentive to stay. I wanted to provide a proportion of the benefits parallel to the proportion of their work time. My boss would not buy it, even though he does not want to lose these workers either. Do other directors of human resources find the same thing happening?

A   Yes. That is a generous offer. Did you also factor the total cost vis-á-vis the contribution? Perhaps there is a compromise in company stock or another strategy which is less expensive but can be tied into the benefits as an incentive idea. As is obvious to benefits managers, not offering benefits is a true cost saving to companies.

Q   We have an awkward situation in our company. The company sits next to the health maintenance organization (HMO) we use. It is a good HMO and the employees are aware of its quality. Our employees can walk right over, be seen, and be back on their lunch hour. However, we do not offer part-time and temporary workers any health care. Now we have so many part-timers one of them has come to me to see if he can use the HMO. He is willing to pay but he wants to pay through the company since it is less costly to him personally. Actually, I do not mind, but will this create a problem for us?

A   Yes and no. Yes, unless you offer the same to all employees. No, if you do make it a universal offer and keep very accurate records. Make sure it does not become an in-kind service on which taxes must be paid.

Q   What other problems might I anticipate with this situation with the part-timer and the HMO?

A Other workers will want the same benefit and well they should. Avoid discrimination by offering the same to all employees or you could be cited. The amount of paperwork may escalate for your own office. On the other hand, it can be used as a great incentive. While it is a creative idea, make sure it is well thought out before implementation.

Q What should I tell this employee regarding use of our HMO? He is waiting to see a physician at the HMO and is impatient to arrange the visit.

A Tell him you think it is a creative idea with merit, but the decision would also influence other employees, part-time as well as full-time. For that reason, your company needs to explore the ramifications of such a decision before the company and the employee can agree. Avoid letting him use the service until you are sure it is OK with the company. Meanwhile, find several other physicians in the area to whom you might refer him; usually a list of three referrals does the trick.

Q If we do go ahead with this idea and he purchases health care on his own, will I need to offer him the option of continuing purchase just like I would with other full-time employees with the benefit?

A Yes. On paper it will appear as a benefit from the company. When he falls into the same categories as other employees who have the same benefit he also comes under the same regulations.

Q We have so many more part-time employees now, yet, because they do not come under our health care program, I am never sure of their health. I can't really encourage them to get care since we won't cover it; it's not the same. Nevertheless, several of our employees do not look well. Is there anything I can do?

A   The only avenues you have for apparent health problems are two routes. You can approach an obvious problem in terms of the environmental health of your work force and for the company. However, unless the presumed problem is interfering with competent work, you cannot address it.

Q   Is there anything else to do with part-timers?

A   You can always make health a work force issue, and discuss it, communicate about it, and provide information about your concerns where employees will see it. Make sure changes are implemented for all employees in a universal manner.

Q   What about the AIDS issue?

A   Unless you know a worker is in danger, or the health of either the worker or others is at risk, you cannot overtly address this issue. The employee—full- or part-time—has rights of confidentiality and you are acting on a presumption.

Q   One of these part-time workers is constantly sneezing on others, leaves dirty handkerchiefs around, and is, in general, not a clean individual. Her work is good, however. Can I do anything about the health issue, as she was willing to see our company physician?

A   Just how good is the work? You need to weigh the effect of this individual on your company, the employees, and the general atmosphere in balance with what you describe. Is this a part-time situation with a set deadline, or, are there other ramifications? Good counseling is always an option, but be careful of how it is handled. However, if she sees the company physician for other than an on-site emergency, since she is not covered—from what you imply—the result may become problematic since it could set a precedent regarding the provision of services to noncovered employees.

Q Last week one of our part-time employees felt dizzy and he was afraid he would faint. I told him to go see our company nurse practitioner. However, since part-timers do not get health care coverage, several of the regular and full-time employees have casually asked me about this action. They think it was inappropriate; was it?

A Not if it was an emergency, as it appears. You are also liable if any employee falls and injures him- or herself on the job. Precaution and prevention are quite different in an emergency than is offering a part-time employee health coverage. Continued service would be another matter, as would follow-up on-site.

Q I am not quite sure about the extent of coverage for part-timers who do not receive health care coverage under our benefits program. Today a woman hurt her arm in the company cafeteria and went to the health service near us. She charged the services received for health care to our company. It this appropriate?

A You need to differentiate between offering health care benefits and workers being injured on the job. Worker's compensation may come into play and needs to be addressed in a different manner. Perhaps this service, as a resolution, may avert a potential larger and legal problem later.

Q Would it work to try to recruit some good administrators with good company health care benefits? A colleague of mine says there are some good administrators out there who are willing to volunteer, even part-time. I find this hard to believe. Is it true?

A Not in great numbers. However, among those workers who are volunteering to work in part-time positions, administrators do make up a larger proportion than almost any other position category. Among females, administrative volunteering is largest with 2.5 percent—albeit, not a large percentage (Piacentini and Foley 1992).

Q We are a very specialized company with a product line that requires a lot of training, even for part-timers or temps. In order to keep a full complement of part-time workers, and not lose all that training time, we have been thinking of offering the part-timers some portion of our health care benefits as a recruitment strategy. We think we may move into the wellness or health promotion sector. Would this work?

A Yes. You need to think about offering it to all in a universal way to avoid discrimination claims. And, you might want to assess the influence on full-timers who may have similar offerings. You would probably want to continue to differentiate between the benefits for full- and part-timers to reward the full-time employee.

Q We have an active group of part-timers who are of retirement age. They love to work, but they are also expressing concern that they are not appreciated. One is interested in more retirement pension added to her benefits. Is this worth exploring?

A Other companies, too, are increasing the numbers of part-timers, temps, and volunteers, to save money. This may need to be assessed individually since too much added in may affect the overall retirement package including social security. If it keeps a good worker on the force—and it sounds as if it might—it is worth the investment. Can you ask for a one-year commitment, for example?

Q I find several of our part-time workers turn down our health care. Is this typical of smaller companies like ours? We have 11 employees.

A Yes. Among smaller companies, there is a greater proportion that will turn down benefits offered (EBRI 1987). It is assumed to be due to the larger number of part-timers and women working in smaller companies.

Q We are in the retail business and hire a lot of women. We currently do not offer health care to our part-timers and we do not want to. It does not seem to be a problem for my other colleagues in retailing, but the women in our small company are upset. Where are we on this one?

A You are in the majority in your industry. Retailing is one of the industries that tends not to offer health care to part-timers; less than a third of the retail companies offered it (EBRI 1987).

Q What about the other industries?

A The types of industries offering health care to part-timers tend to be the wholesale trade, manufacturing, and finance companies (EBRI 1987).

Q What percentage of these companies offer health care to part-timers?

A In these three industries, over 70 percent offer some form of health care benefit (EBRI 1987).

TEMPORARY EMPLOYEES

Q   We have been using a number of temporary workers or temps as employees lately. We are a manufacturing company and find we need to rely on them an increasing amount. However, we do not want to offer them benefits. Are we required to?

A   Not at this time. Under reform all workers will be addressed, but currently the temp is not included.

Q   What is the national trend for employment in the category of temporary worker?

A   According to reports published by the National Association of Temporary Services (Uchitelle 1993, p. A1), the number of temps increased from 224,000 in 1992 to 348,000 in 1993.

Q   In order to cut costs in manufacturing and to cover for potential loss and intermittent job orders, we are using more temporary workers. Do most other firms offer benefits to these workers?

A   No. Most do not offer them health care benefits. However, some firms do offer a worker compensation package and, of course, social security (Uchitelle 1993, p. A1).

Q   A lot of our temps are women. We are becoming convinced that there is rampant discrimination against this group of workers. Are there any data to substantiate these perceptions?

A   There are two issues that you raise, gender and discrimination. First, among temporary workers there is a larger proportion of females although the proportions are shifting toward a balance. The second question pertaining to discrimination is also correct. Historically, reports have been based more on males than females, suggesting a potential bias against females in both actuarial data as well as in reports regarding the insurance market (Harrington 1985).

Q The more temps we hire in our offices the more the other workers become disgruntled. We thought we should make it clear the temp does not get benefits. Would this help to appease the regular workers?

A Maybe. It will depend on the manner in which it is done and the actual issues among these groups. If, however, all workers end up with some benefit, then it is a moot issue. You might just anger the temps into requesting benefits. Handle carefully.

Q Because we do not offer any benefits to temporary workers in our various companies, my boss is anxious for us to hire more as a cost-saving strategy. This has created a situation where the regular workers, both full- and part-timers, are coming in to find out if we plan to drop all health care benefits. I know if we did we would lose several of our best workers. This seems like a lose–lose situation. How can we turn it around?

A A direct communication to the regular workers stating health care benefits will not be dropped might suffice. If not completely resolved, follow up with a few conversations with leaders and key personnel in your informal network among those same workers.

Q An employee came to see me because he cut his arm while at work on the assembly line. He does not receive any worker's compensation and is a temp worker, so we do not cover health care. He is quite angry and thinks he may complain. What do others do in these situations?

A Establish a clear policy that distinguishes between a work-related injury and health care coverage and benefits. Provision of emergency care and attention to injuries is the key issue. Avert a larger problem while you can.

Q Is it true company size makes a difference in whether health care is offered to part-time and temporary employees?

A Yes. The larger firms are found to have "restrictive requirements" and consequently are more likely to exclude their temporary and part-timers (EBRI 1987).

Q Sometimes I spend a great deal of time working out a benefits plan for a temp worker and then the worker leaves. I want to stop offering health care benefits in a month, but my boss is not convinced it is a good plan. What are the trends?

A The key trend is away from benefits for part-timers and temps, and more hire of those worker categories. Your point is well made: Calculation of cost is not only in the direct cost; indirect cost of administration is also a large factor.

Q We seem to always be in need of new workers, and my boss is trying to cut down on costs, as is everyone else. We have one company in a small area where a lot of women volunteer. He thinks the company's recruitment will be enhanced if we seek more temps who are volunteers (who work without pay), and then offer them some minimum health care benefits. Is this a feasible plan?

A   Fewer companies are offering benefits to part-timers and temps as noted earlier, and even fewer to volunteers. However, it may surprise you to learn that volunteers working part-time made up almost 15 percent of the work force in 1991 (Piacentini and Foley 1992).

Q   Can I assume more of those volunteers are women rather than men?

A   Yes. Gender difference is an accurate assumption. Among volunteers in companies, the proportions were 4.2 percent and 10.3 percent male and female, respectively (Piacentini and Foley 1992).

Q   Although we have several workers on our force who are temps, they work full-time. In fact, in one instance a temporary is one of our most valued employees. We have offered her a full-time regular job but she declines. She likes flexibility. Would it help to offer her benefits?

A   Ask if she would be willing to join your company as a full-time permanent employee with specific benefits; find out what she values. You will need to assess the difference between what she wants and what you currently offer to other full-time employees. The difference may not be worth the investment. Your first question is what is desirable to her about remaining as a temporary employee. Until you can answer the question regarding her preferences, benefits are a moot issue.

Q   We tend to hire a lot of temps because we are in a university town and get good temporary workers who are students. Our full-timers seem to resent this. We do not offer the students (temps) any benefits so they are quite cost-effective. Nevertheless, we wonder if it would be worth it to communicate about lack of benefits to the other employees?

A What you are describing is a preventive damage control strategy. It sounds as if it would be worthwhile to let the informal communication system work for you on this one. One wonders if the benefits generate this resentment or whether it is the college education. Do you know for sure which it is?

Q We have an agency that gets us good temps for a variety of situations. However, we found out what the agency actually pays the workers is about 40 percent of what we pay. We are thinking of using benefits as an attractive means of getting them to go direct with us. It would be more cost-effective for us and for them. Several of the workers have complained about the low pay and the negative attitude of the agency. Is this too hot to touch?

A It is a sensitive issue. However, make sure your temp employees do not have a clause or a contract regarding working with the same client if they go out of contract. Will you need the agency in the future? Benefits as a retention item is an old issue but it may need to be reassessed in light of the complexity of this situation. Even so, use the informal mechanisms in your organization to obtain data on this situation, and avoid written communication about the inquiries.

REFERENCES

Employee Benefits Research Institute (EBRI). 1987. *Government Mandating of Employee Benefits*. Washington, D.C.: EBRI.

Harrington, G. 1985. *The Health Insurance Fact & Answer Book*. New York: Harper & Row.

Piacentini, J., and Foley, J. 1992. *EBRI Databook on Employee Benefits, 2nd ed.* Washington, D.C.: Employee Benefits Research Institute.

Scott, A. 1993. Part-time work. *The Almanac* 26(30): 1.

Uchitelle, L. 1993. Use of temporary workers is on rise in manufacturing. *New York Times,* 6 July: A1.

Worker's compensation: Tactics for cutting costs. *Nation's Business,* 79(4): 33.

11

Retirement Packages for Employees

Retirement benefits have long been viewed as an employee right, and changes in retiree benefits pose many challenges for the director of human resources. This chapter explores a number of pressing problems directors face when needing to address changes in the retirement packages of their company's current employees and the recent retirees. Solutions are presented to address these numerous challenges. Strategies are discussed paralleling the current trends in health care benefits.

Q We need to trim our retirement packages. What are other companies doing to trim?

A A great deal depends on what you mean by the term *trim*. In some instances, trim is a code word for reduction to the point of elimination. In some cases, it means modest adjustments. You need to assess what your company needs and consider where you want to be in, for example, five years. Long-range planning should be your target.

Q It seems to us in the human resource field there is nothing more touchy than the retirement package of a longtime employee. Is it worth addressing reductions in retirement or would my company be better off to look elsewhere for cost cuts in health care benefits?

A You are right about your perception. Like social security, this issue deeply concerns employees. Before moving ahead, assess in the following ways: Determine how many individuals you have who fall into the retirement category. Examine their positions in the company relative to what you are currently offering them. Would the benefits you offer in health care allow them to retire early, or are you addressing the retiree, who at 65, has other options? Once you know the clear answers to these questions, you are in a much better position to make a firm decision.

Q Is it true that, generally, retiree benefits are being reduced?

A Yes. Over the past several years, the percentage of companies that have reduced their retirement packages for retirees is up from 43 percent in 1989, to 69 percent in 1992 (Freudenheim 1993, p. 17).

Q In terms of actually eliminating retirement packages for retirees, what are companies doing?

A Companies are tending toward an elimination of the retirement package for health care. For example, whereas, in 1989 only 3 percent eliminated health care benefits for their retirees, by 1992 that percent had edged up to 7 percent.

Q We are thinking of increasing the proportion of the benefits package we put into retirement, but we need some comparison data. What is being done?

A   Among firms in 1990, out of the total proportion of monies allocated into benefits as a payroll percentage, about 6 percent was spent on retirement and savings (Piacentini and Foley 1992).

Q   Is there a difference in the amount that employers allocate based on the type of company?

A   While the size and type of company has been an influence in most instances, for benefits contributions it is not (Piacentini and Foley 1992). The data show it is almost exactly the same across all companies and for manufacturing and nonmanufacturing companies.

Q   Which is greater, the contribution that employers make to the retirement, or to the medical benefits?

A   Overall, among all companies the contribution to retirement is a bit more than half the medical benefits contribution for all categories of medical benefits (Piacentini and Foley 1992).

Q   An employee came to see me today and said that she had been reading a book on benefits. She claimed in our industry, which is clothing sales, the benefits for retirement are really low. Is this true?

A   Your employee must be reading the right books. Apparel companies have the smallest contribution to retirement benefits compared to any other industry (Piacentini and Foley 1992). For example, in 1990, apparel was 1.8 percent compared to the high in food, beverages, and tobacco which was 8 percent. The average for the same year was 5.5 percent.

Q   We want to increase the proportional amount of benefits we allocate to retirement. However, my CEO is running scared about the next century in terms of occurring future liability which is now required of companies as they project future payout for retirement funds. Is this a smart change to make?

A   It may be a smart change but perhaps not at this time. You need more data to see what your total projected costs—including liability—will be. Without those data you cannot make a clear decision.

Q   Is there a trend in terms of size reflected in reducing or eliminating the retirement package?

A   Yes. Smaller companies appear to be moving first, although the trends reflected in studies indicate companies of various sizes are doing so.

Q   What are some of the ways companies are saving money in health care retirement packages?

A   Among companies continuing to offer a retirement package, the increase in contribution requested from the retirees for their health care benefits is the primary means of reducing costs (Piacentini and Foley 1992).

Q   What is the trend reflected in this strategy for reducing company costs?

A   Thirty percent have implemented increase of retiree contribution as a strategy (Freudenheim 1993, p. 17).

Q   What are the trends for the immediate future?

A   In addition to the 30 percent that have implemented increased contributions, another 28 percent plan to in the near future (Freudenheim 1993, p. 17).

Q   What other strategies are used by firms to reduce the costs of retiree health care benefits?

A   Out-of-pocket payment increases or deductible increases for the retirees are implemented by 21 percent of those companies offering health care benefits to retirees (Freudenheim 1993, p. 17).

Q   In terms of other strategies to reduce retiree costs in benefits, what are businesses planning for the next several years?

A   Slightly fewer planned to increase the deductible or the out-of-pocket payment: 18 percent (Freudenheim 1993, p. 17).

Q   Is it true tightening eligibility is being implemented by firms nationally?

A   Yes. Among those firms currently offering health care benefits to their employees who have retired, roughly 11 percent implemented a tougher eligibility requirement in either 1991 or 1992 (Freudenheim 1993, p. 17).

Q   Will more companies tighten eligibility criteria?

A   More—13 percent—are planning to initiate an eligibility strategy than have actually implemented a tightened criterion (Freudenheim 1993, p. 17).

Q   We as a company know the retiree health care benefits are an emotional issue for many workers. Why is this?

A   It is, indeed, a hot topic among workers. It is especially so for those loyal workers who have stayed with a company that offered retiree health care benefits and whose company then reduced those planned benefits.

Q Are there regulations that mitigate against dropping retirees' health care?

A At this current time, health care is not required for retirees. Check for current and changing laws, however.

Q Can we drop health care benefits for those former employees who have already retired? Won't this get us into trouble?

A The question is, what change does this represent? Your question suggests the employee retired with the benefits in place and then you eliminate the benefits. If you treat all former employees alike, you are in the appropriate position.

Q Is there any reason we cannot reduce the company-offered health care employee benefits for retirees?

A A number of court cases in the early 1990s upheld the right of a firm to reduce the employer's package for retirement health care benefits (Freudenheim 1993, p. 17).

Q What are employers' perspectives on this issue of health care benefits for retirees?

A Apparently, according to reports on the matter, there is diversity among employers and thus their companies regarding this issue (Freudenheim 1993, p. 17).

Q What influences the perception of companies on health care for retirees?

A Several factors influence the viewpoint held by a firm. Among them is the overall environment in which the company is based, the wage range, and the market (Freudenheim 1993, p. 17).

Q   Does the type of industry affect the approach to reduction of health care benefits costs for retirees?

A   Yes. Those with fewer retirees, the newer companies in high-tech industries, prefer a flat premium, whereas a payroll tax is preferred by the auto industry, for example, which has a larger number of retirees (Freudenheim 1993, p. 17).

Q   What federal regulations do I need to be concerned with in terms of retirees' health care benefits?

A   None at this time; benefits are not mandatory for those who retire.

Q   Is there any way in which one should think about changes in retirees' benefits as different from other benefits? Are there some specific factors pertaining to the retiree groups of employees that are significantly different from other employee groups?

A   Yes, in the sense that all employees know or assume that some day, in the future, they will retire and not work. Most employees look at the retirement package much like social security: It is a right earned. So, with this difference in mind, you do need to treat this group in a slightly different way. Even though younger employees may not be in this group, they assume that someday they will be. The next group to be concerned about is the near-retiree group, the ones soon coming into this category. If you have an intergroup problem among your employees, you can anticipate that the retiree and about-to-retire group will join forces.

Q   How expensive is the retiree group in terms of health care?

A   The answer depends on the health of your group and the number that occupy the retiree category. However, remember that in terms of just one disease such as cancer, the number of claims increases with age alone. Therefore, age is always a factor in health care costs: The older are more costly.

Q   Yesterday one of my employees came in to talk with me about his health care. It seems that he was recently diagnosed with a chronic and potentially fatal disease. He is thinking about retiring early and taking his current benefits package with him. He is aware our company may cut retirement packages in the near future and he wants to bow out while he can with as much of his health care package as possible. What should I tell him?

A   Do you know what the company is going to do? You can only tell him what you know to be the actual situation. You can tell him that retirement is not required in the provisions and may be cut; retirement benefits are not guaranteed. However, with governmental reform it may be more accessible to him in the future.

Q   It is my analysis as a human resource director that retirement is a large proportion of our increase in benefits. How do we compare to other companies?

A   Surveys have found two categories accounted for most of the increase in benefits costs: medical and retirement plans (Thompson 1993a, p. 38).

Q   On average, what do companies usually contribute to the average retirement plans?

A   In 1992, according to surveys, employers contributed about 6 percent to all types of retirement plans (Thompson 1993a, p. 38).

Q   The annual contribution amount that employers make for retirement seems higher than in previous years. Has there been an increase?

A   Yes, the amount in 1989 was 5.1 percent, in 1990 it was 5.5 percent, and in 1991, the latest figures from a national survey, it was 6.0 percent of the annual company budget (Thompson 1993a, p. 38).

Q   We have given some thought to eliminating our retirement package altogether. How prevalent is this move?

A   The number of companies that are reducing or eliminating their retirement packages continues to grow. For instance, in a national survey, it was found that in 1991 about 16.4 percent of companies did not offer any retirement. This reflects an increase from the previous year of 15.2 percent without retirement packages (Thompson 1993a, p. 38).

Q   The newly mandated future projected liability of our company for the projected costs of employees' retirement benefits is one of our greatest concerns in terms of health care benefits.

A   Yes. Your concern is well substantiated by the $412 billion reported by the General Accounting Office which reflects a current increase from 1989, when it was $227 billion (Freudenheim 1993, p. 17).

Q   We are a nonmanufacturing company. What is the average for retirement benefits costs in this sector of business?

A   According to a 1991 survey, the nonmanufacturing benefits cost was 39.4 percent as a percentage of the payroll, which represented an average of $12,761 per individual employee as an annual average benefits cost (Thompson 1993a, p. 38).

Q   My CEO came to me and told me about the new regulations for retirees. As the director of human resources for my company, I need now to plan ahead to comply with these new federal regulations. What can we do?

A   Obtain the health claims of all retirees in your company over the past five years, average them, add in a projected escalation of health care costs based on current figures which are approximately 6 percent per year. Add these in and project them as a base for future retiree benefits into the next decade.

Q   We want to continue to offer a retirement package for our employees, but we also have the idea that, nationally, there is a decline in pension packages. How do we compare with other companies?

A   In a survey conducted on pension plans, only 42 percent of American workers had an employer-sponsored plan in place. A decline is projected in this 42 percent as well (Thompson 1993b, p. 57).

Q   Is there a difference in the size of the company? We are relatively small and think that we may do away with our pension plan.

A   Yes. A Small Business Administration survey found in the years between 1986 and 1990, at least one plan among those offered by companies was eliminated by the 29 percent of companies that offered any pension plans (Thompson 1993b, p. 57).

Q Are there other ways in which size of the company will influence the plan?

A Yes. Company size also influences the type of plan offered for retirement. For example, of the companies that were smallest, the majority also offered a defined-contribution plan (Thompson 1993b, p. 57). That type of plan is one to which the employee and the employer contribute. In contrast, the larger firms tended to offer a defined-benefit plan which is geared to salary and the years of service to that employer.

Q Does size influence whether a plan is offered?

A Yes. The smaller the company, for example, those under 24 employees, also had the smallest amount of those employees covered with 12.8 percent (Thompson 1993b, p. 57). Those companies with over 500 employees had 81.8 percent coverage for retirement plans. Company size is a key factor in health care retirement plans.

Q We are getting anxious about the IRS program which was adopted in 1991—the closing agreement program (CAP). We do not think we have any pending penalties, but maybe it would be more prudent to simply drop our pension plans. What are other companies doing about this?

A Responses vary. However, if you do not think you have a penalty in the pension area of your benefits package, why drop it? Your employees value pensions (Rowland 1993, p. 14).

Q   I am not clear about the new rule that went into effect in January of 1993 regarding retiree accounts. What should I know?

A   The new rule, approved by the Financial Accounting Standards Board, requires health benefits for retirees to be reflected in a company's benefits and recordkeeping books as a liability. As the director of human resources, you will be required to project these costs as a liability by assuming what your company anticipates in the employee's retirement years. It also means you need to be fairly accurate in projecting costs for the future (Warner 1993, p. 32).

Q   We are a relatively small company, with under 200 employees. Will the new retire rules for projecting costs affect us?

A   Yes, however, national companies with fewer than 500 participants have until January 1 of 1995 to come into compliance with the new ruling (Warner 1993, p. 32).

Q   What is the difference between the new rules on the retire benefits package for health care, and the old way we did things?

A   In the past, most companies retained records or reflected the cost of a retirement pension plan as they were paid out (Warner 1993, p. 32). The new ruling will require that companies reflect a projection of the retirement costs for the future as a liability. In the future, companies will need to reflect retirement benefits as a cost they will be liable to pay.

Q   In order to comply with the new rulings, what will I need to consider and estimate for an accurate projection of future costs?

A At a minimum you should be able to calculate the change in retirement need for health services, Medicare costs and their influence, retirement patterns, and the rules for accounting and how they are linked with health care and its assessment (Warner 1993, p. 32).

Q How can I best prepare for the changes we will face in the retiree arena in the next decade? We have a loyal company work force that has stayed with us, a large proportion of whom will probably retire in the next ten years.

A There are several steps you can take now. Start by getting related data like actuarial figures and age-related information on actual use. Then review the current retiree benefits package that the company offers, and assess it in light of the company portfolio. Ask hard questions, like whether the plan is too large, what does the company owe employees, and can the plan absorb the changes in light of the projected changes in health care? Next you might think of comparing your company's plans with those of existing plans like the current Medicare plans. Lastly, create a plan reflecting the required changes in your firm as well as the current changes in health care nationally. These should start you on the way to a realistic retirement package and assist you in balancing the liability with the current budget.

Q We are a company with a focus on trade. How do we compare with others in our similar field?

A Among all companies focusing on trade, 28.8 percent offered a retirement plan in 1990 (Thompson 1993b, p. 57).

Q As the director of a large human resource program, I am inundated with paperwork. All these federal regulations have me swamped. Am I alone?

A   Not at all. The new federal regulations for retirement and for benefits in general, are a major factor in many companies deciding to drop their retirement coverage. In a recent survey, 61 percent of small firms, which are generally those with fewer than 24 employees, reported that the main reason for terminating a pension plan was "onerous federal laws and regulations."

Q   My company, in which I direct resources for benefits, is small. When I go to meetings and talk with larger companies it seems they manage fairly well. What about the smaller company, about which little is written?

A   You may be correct in your perception. Among smaller companies there is less flexibility in offering benefits because there are fewer employees in the firm across which to spread an expensive outlay. Likewise, it is not possible to have as many options. In general, the larger the firm, the larger the proportion offering benefits (Thompson 1993b, p. 57).

Q   We are preparing for some major cuts in our retirement benefits, and we anticipate a number of complaints from our current employees. What is the status of most retirement funds?

A   According to a *Money* magazine report (Simon 1993, p. 104), over 20 percent of all benefits funds are currently underfunded, based on reports prior to taking cuts.

Q   We think that we are in the ballpark with our retirement package but several of our employees who recently retired are complaining. We are a national firm with slightly over 220 employees. What are the statistics on retirement packages in firms today?

A Among firms with more than 200 employees, only 41 percent of those companies offered health benefits to retirees in the past year (Simon 1993, p. 104).

Q Are these numbers going down?

A Absolutely. With cuts in health care and escalations in services, the trend reflects a current cut from 46 percent in 1991; projection statistics suggest it may drop to a low of 25 percent by the year 2000 (Simon 1993, p. 104).

Q When one reads the current literature on retirement, it seems to indicate that one will need about 80 percent of one's current income on which to retire. Are those statistics transferable to health care and its benefits as well?

A There is not an exact parallel. The percentage of income needed is not the same as the amount projected for health care. In fact, the health care costs of the retiree age group are higher than for the working population. Current estimates, using conservative, postreform figures, suggest about 20 percent of retiree income will go to medical expenses (Simon 1993, p. 113).

Q Do we have to continue to offer employees and our retirees who leave the option to purchase health care coverage, even though we will not pay for it?

A Yes, COBRA law requires a firm to offer an employee the option of purchasing through their company's group coverage after leaving the company (Simon 1993, p. 113).

Q Are there some creative solutions to the problem of keeping good employees, cutting their retirement benefits, and retaining our own budget base?

A   There are several. Retirees of one firm were given some company stock in a recent settlement where benefits were reduced and, in some instances, cut (AP 1993, p. C3). The cuts were originally made because of the rising medical care costs as well as liability for retirement insurance as a result of recent regulations.

Q   In an effort to improve the communication between our office and the about-to-retire group, I met with employees—about 15. We discussed their wishes for retirement. I was astounded to find that they wanted long-term care included. What about this?

A   It should come as no surprise that employees would want such coverage. Long-term care coverage is among the fastest growing sectors of the health care industry (*Hospitals & Health Networks* 1993, p. 60) and is also one of the most costly.

Q   For some reason our retirees are concerned about something called the continuum of care. Why is this?

A   Continuum of care refers to the seamless offering of health care services across a number of different types of service (for example, going from a hospital back to the nursing home or a community facility). Because of massive restructuring of health care facilities which involves the merger of different types of facilities and services, continuity of care, or its lack, has become an increasingly common problem in health care.

Q   Why is this so much of an issue for retirees?

A   Older people tend to have a higher health care facility use. The elderly as a group, who have heightened use of numbers of facilities across a continuum of care, pay special attention to this issue since it affects them in greater proportion and to a greater degree than other age groups. Therefore, retirees who may fall into this age group have more concerns for continuity of care than others.

Q   Are other companies considering long-term care as a coverage item in the benefits package for retirees?

A   Although figures vary on this point, the trend is toward reduction, not expansion.

Q   An employee is very concerned about the high incidence of cancer in her family. She recently came in to discuss the possibility of getting catastrophic illness coverage. I don't think this is wise. What should she be told?

A   This situation raises several issues. The first is whether you want to offer this for just this employee, or whether you plan to offer it to other employees. Without the foundation of a flexible or menu-type benefits plan, you may get cited for discrimination if it is not offered to all employees. Second, look at the facts and statistics on this type of coverage. Generally, questions are raised about whether they are a sound investment for one's dollars. Third, encourage this employee to obtain a comprehensive medical evaluation as a preventive step.

Q   I understand that several of our soon-to-retire employees are quite disturbed about the possibility of major changes in their retirement benefits. What can I do to avert this kind of hostility in our company?

A   Several ideas come to mind. The first is preventive. Provide your employees with data on the costs of the current program. Show them how it influences the company overall.

Q   What else can we do?

A   If data alone do not address the whole problem, it will go a long way if it is coupled with a discussion and continuing information. In addition, get statistics—like those provided in this book—reflecting the current trends nationally and among other companies that are similar to yours. This information and the approach should support your position and back your ultimate decision.

Q   What strategies are companies using to limit costs for retirees?

A   According to government reports, companies are doing one of three things. Firms are asking retirees to pay more into the company, limiting medical services, and/or restricting who is covered (U.S. General Accounting Office 1989, p. 11).

Q   What are companies doing in terms of limiting coverage?

A   Eligibility may be limited in terms of the defined age an employee must reach to be covered, and the total years of employment that an employee must have for benefits coverage to take effect (U.S. General Accounting Office 1989, p. 11).

Q   Are there other strategies firms are using?

A   In addition to the above, they are also reducing the age for stopping eligibility, and stating if and for how long dependents, including spouses, may be covered (U.S. General Accounting Office 1989, p. 12).

Q   Is it true we could limit or eliminate a portion of our health care plan?

A   Yes. And companies are doing just that to reduce costs (U.S. General Accounting Office 1989, p. 13).

Q   We are considering other cost-containment measures. Can we mandate regulatory measures?

A   Yes, indeed. Companies are currently using more utilization reviews, increasing the number and scope of mandatory second opinions, as well as increasing hospital preadmission certifications (U.S. General Accounting Office 1989, p. 14). All of these cut costs.

Q   Are there figures on the difference it makes to a company when copayments are increased?

A   Yes. For example, in government studies a company not requiring contributions paid out about $4,000 annually per retiree (U.S. General Accounting Office 1989, p. 14). In contrast, when contributions were increased the amount was reduced to about $2,040 for employee and dependent per year, and to $1,020 for the employee alone per year. These are significant savings.

Q   Are there different ways for attaining cost-containment that companies are using? What are some of these?

A   One way is to reduce the amount the company will pay out when the retiree reaches the age for Medicare to begin (U.S. General Accounting Office 1989, p. 14).

Q   We think we will restrict the amount of a retiree's medical expenses that our plan will pay. Is this appropriate?

A   The strategy is being used and is effective (U.S. General Accounting Office 1989, p. 14). As to its appropriateness, that needs to be assessed for your company, but others are doing it.

Q   Is it true companies are also getting retirees on plans to pay a specified dollar amount before health care expenses will be paid for by the company plan?

A   Yes, and it does work. It is proving to be an effective strategy (U.S. General Accounting Office 1989, p. 12).

Q   An employee came in to talk to me about his pending retirement. His major concern, as you can imagine, was health care. He said we do not have a restriction clause in our plan's statement and he assumed we would not change it. Is this accurate?

A   No. While a company may not have a current restriction clause pertaining to changing their health care plans for retirees, in prior court cases a company was upheld when it made changes even without such language.

Q   Is there an example of such a situation?

A   Yes. In the lawsuit involving the Grand Trunk Western Railroad Company, the rail company had the right to change even without ". . . explicit language reserving the right . . ." to change (U.S. General Accounting Office 1989, p. 12).

Q   We do not have language to cover us in our plans. Would it be smart to put it in?

A   Yes. As a precaution it would be prudent to insert language covering your company in such instances. Even though the court has upheld companies in the past, attitudes may change.

Q   What have other companies done?

A   In government reports, the majority of companies have language to cover them. Of the few that do not, they have added contingency language (U.S. General Accounting Office 1989, p. 13).

Q Does it help to review on a regular basis?

A Absolutely. Other companies are providing a thorough review of the situation on a regular, routine basis. This works as a prevention as well as a planning device (U.S. General Accounting Office 1989, p. 14).

Q We are really concerned. Our firm has a lot of employees who are nearing retirement age. If we have to assume their liability for retirement costs as a projected amount, it will be enormous, and all in one year. Is there anything we can do?

A Short of dropping retirement you have several optional strategies. One would be to limit amount of time covered by retirement, specify certain coverage, or limit ages on certain employer contributions. You should examine your package carefully, since any change will be construed as a reduction in the present package. Assess the impact on current employees.

Q What if we cannot take on the amount of liability we will need in order to project future retirement amounts? What then?

A Assess and project as tightly as possible. Then plan for phased-in retirements, set priorities on full and partial packages with employee categories and allocate using those principles. Perhaps you do not need to provide a full package to all employees.

Q Do any firms allow their employees to elect not to take their retirement? How does it work?

A Some, but only a few firms allow employees under a flexible benefits plan to elect to not participate. Usually it is a woman with a husband who is well-covered on another company's plan.

Q What happens to those benefits? Wouldn't it actually be good to have several of these?

A Yes. Given the projected plans for retirements, it may be a cost saving to trade off retirement with its inherent liability with current bonuses, stock options, or other selections. Make sure the selection is attractive to the employee and does not incur additional liability as a future projected cost.

Q A female employee came in to question the way we were allocating our retirement benefits. She argued that women are less often covered by retirement health coverage than are men. Is this true?

A Unfortunately, she is correct. Although the percentages are quite similar, men are actually covered in greater proportion than women, 49 to 41 percent (Piacentini and Foley 1992), respectively.

Q Is gender also an issue regarding employees not covered?

A Surveys find that among employees not covered by retirement health coverage, females outnumber males 30 to 22 percent (Piacentini and Foley 1992).

Q Is it true some retirees are getting into specialized HMO arrangements with a collaborative relationship between the HMO and Medicare?

A   Yes. This is quite new and currently being studied. HMOs that enroll retirees and replace the Medicare coverage are receiving a small monthly fee from Medicare. It would be worth exploring these as a complement to the employer benefits package that your company offers (Watkins et al. 1992, p. 310).

Q   How is the fee calculated, and how would it affect benefits?

A   How it would affect benefits is unclear except Medicare calculates the fees it pays to the HMO based on a fixed percentage of costs from fee-for-service. Not considered is health status (Watkins et al. 1992, p. 310).

Q   Is it true that some of the HMOs have been accused of selection bias?

A   Questions have been raised about the HMOs receiving favorable selection bias on the part of some federal representatives. These questions are aimed at the HMO's marketing efforts. However, a study was conducted using 10,035 Medicare recipients among 20 HMOs that did not validate all those claims (Watkins et al. 1992, p. 311).

REFERENCES

AP. 1993. Company news. *New York Times*, 1 July: C3.

Freudenheim, M. 1993. Health limbo for early retirees. *New York Times*, 10 July: 17.

Home care: Robust growth continues. 1993. *Hospitals & Health Networks*, 20 June: 60.

Piacentini, J. and Foley, J. 1992. *EBRI Databook on Employee Benefits, 2nd ed.* Washington, D.C.: Employee Benefits Research Institute.

Rowland, M. 1993. IRS sharpens pension plan knife. *New York Times*, 4 July: Sec. 3: 14.

Simon, R. 1993. How to retire early. *Money* 22(6): 102–113.

Thompson, R. 1993a. Benefits update: Benefits costs surge again. *Nation's Business*, February: 38.

Thompson, R. 1993b. A decline in covered workers. *Nation's Business*, March: 57.

U.S. General Accounting Office. 1989. *Employee Benefits: Company Actions to Limit Retiree Health Costs*, February: 11–14.

Warner, D. 1993. Accounting-rule change. *Nation's Business* 79(4): 32.

Watkins, B., et al. 1992. HMO advertising and enrollee health status: Marketing Medicare plans to seniors. *Health Communication* 4(4): 303–322.

12

Preventing Problems

As all directors of human resources know, health care benefits problems can be a costly challenge, often contributing to the loss of company profit. Proactive administration of health care resources can prevent problems before they emerge. Resourceful administration not only saves in term of dollars and cents, but increases the productivity and motivation of employees and their companies. This chapter discusses ways to think through today's problems and their solutions with an eye to prevention; to seek ways to avert similar problems in the future. Critical to this process is information collected today to avoid problems in the next century. As with health care in general, the lessons of the twentieth century highlight prevention as less costly than cure. Strategies raised in this section will alert the savvy director of health benefits to proactive ways to predict and thereby avoid health care benefits problems in the future.

TRENDS FOR PREVENTION

Q Given the trends for the twenty-first century, where should we focus today?

A On prevention, on health, and on cost-effective ways to achieve them for your company. You cannot lose with this combination.

Q What can we do to anticipate problems to prevent liability buildup, especially with our retirees?

A Retiree benefits are anticipated to be a costly aspect well into the twenty-first century. To prevent further problems do as others are doing: Restrict for age or length of coverage, specify qualifiers for particular coverage, and plan well in advance.

Q Our employees are beginning to understand the need for the current changes. What can we do to encourage them and keep our momentum?

A Set up a continuous flow of communication and feedback so mechanisms are in place to anticipate change as well as plan for them. Some firms are using, for example, joint employee–manager discussion groups for ongoing direct communication. These will keep your company current and in touch with your employees.

Q We want to continue to use our health care benefits to retain employees. What can we do to prevent the problems of loss we incurred in the past?

A The use of employee networks and continuous monitoring will be fruitful. Include in your networks both retirees as well as current employees. Include employees with ability to look to the future.

Q What can we do to keep our company viable in terms of preventing problems in the future?

A   Assess the trends in a continuous way and project your plans for at least five years. Then, reassess in light of the changes needed now for the five-year plans; assess for disparity, then change.

Q   Would using a consultant aid us in retaining employees and remaining viable in terms of preventing problems in health care?

A   It might. If you hired a consultant with knowledge of health care reform as well as benefits you could keep current.

Q   Is it true in the area of part-timers and temp workers there will be dramatic changes? How can we prevent problems?

A   The dramatic changes anticipated have to do with reform in health care and the increasing use of part-timers and temps. Since access for all workers will be seen in health care reform, this employee category will probably see dramatic changes.

Q   Our company has a fine reputation in the community as a company with solid benefits. What can we do to continue with our health care program?

A   You can become more selective in criteria for coverage, specify in more detail, reduce the length of time the benefits are in effect for retirees, and state in clear language that you may need to change. The latter should be in effect now.

Q   How long do trendsetters predict downsizing will continue?

A   No one can be absolutely sure, but if suggestions are correct, project well through the first decade of the next century.

Q I think retirement benefits are going to be important future considerations. Am I right?

A You are absolutely right in terms of preventing problems for the future. With the issues of retirement liability looming on the horizon, a savvy director of human resources can save his or her company large sums of money—and a large headache—by accurately predicting the company's retirement picture into the next century. In terms of prevention, avoid this problem area by using conservative estimates and allowing for some leeway in the future.

Q If I were going to look into a crystal ball and try to avoid problems in say, ten years, where should I focus?

A On the retirement package, on the overall package promised to current employees, and to the amount of deductible that employees are asked to share. Add in the ability to analyze with current data. With close attention to these factors, a company should be able to manage.

Q What are the major features in planning for the future?

A A major feature is the final outcome of health care reform. How reform evolves over the next several years, not just now, will have an enormous influence on the company bottom line. Also, explore the types of health care delivery models developed as a response to pending reform.

Q Do you think health care benefits will continue?

A Yes, but not in the same shape in which they exist now. They will be responsive to changes, flexible, and cost restrained. And, they will parallel the health care reforms projected for the mid- to late 1990s.

Q Will managed competition survive?

A Although it may not be called managed competition, some form of service system that allows both employers and employees to participate in a health care system that is more cost-effective than what we currently have is a given.

Q Is it true the current fee-for-service system will not be available in the twenty-first century?

A Although reduction is projected, many physicians hope it will not be the case—at least not to the point of total elimination.

NEW APPROACHES

Q Several people in our field have suggested one way to eliminate overhead costs would be to use more of the extended-care providers. Is this correct?

A They are probably referring to the phenomenon of using expanded roles professional nurses are developing. For example, the nurse practitioner with an emphasis in family care, psychiatric care, or medical care could provide a wide range of preventive and treatment services at less cost than physicians. The use of these providers would then free physicians for higher-risk patients.

Q What would be the implication for our benefits if more expanded-care providers were used?

A A dramatic cost saving. Expanded-care practitioners are not paid at the same rate as a physician, although they do offer similar services for lower-risk patients.

Q We think the quality of care that nurse practitioners offer would not be as good as that of our regular physicians. Is this true?

A It depends on what you mean. Nurse practitioners have a very high quality rating in comparison to physicians, however, they do not perform all the services that physicians perform. Within the parameters of their practice they are, according to well-designed studies (*Journal of the American Academy of Nurse Practitioners* 1990, p. 93), of comparable—and in some instances higher—quality in terms of care delivery and consumer satisfaction. Do not discount these health care providers.

Q I understand one reason that nurse practitioners are so popular is they emphasize prevention. True?

A Yes. Generally, nursing has a greater emphasis on prevention than has medicine. Nurse practitioners emphasize prevention and education.

Q Would it be wise to get a nurse practitioner to run our wellness programs or our EAPs? It would save us money.

A Absolutely. These types of programs are practically designed for the expanded roles in health care providers that nurse practitioners exemplify. With an emphasis on prevention, low-risk consumers, and education, these programs would be an excellent match. Keep a physician referral for high-risk situations.

Q Will physician assistants continue to function as care providers?

A Probably, especially in rural areas with limited access. These types of providers may be a boon to small companies that have limited services or options in small communities, in low-access areas, or sparsely populated areas of the country.

Q   How can I prevent hostility from developing between our part- and full-time employees regarding health care benefits? We rely on both these groups.

A   This is an excellent example of a place in which prevention is a good strategy. Put some energy into working with both the part-timer and the full-timer as groups, affirming the particular contributions both make. Point out why the benefits are designed as they are, but get your facts in order before meeting with them. Especially important to positive relationships between the two groups is affirmation of their interdependence. Perhaps they are not clear on how the part-timers assist the full-time employees and the responsibility full-timers take on within the total company, which is an asset for the part-timers. Some conversation about mutual roles and overall benefits would be healthy for the company.

Q   We think a program putting more emphasis on prevention in health care would, in the long run, decrease our claims. Any facts on this for larger companies?

A   The shift into prevention is an excellent plan, however, it is also a relatively new phenomenon in company benefits programming nationally. Thus, statistics are still coming in.

Q   Are there creative examples of insured programs focusing on prevention?

A   One of the first nontraditional programs emphasizing prevention is a "heart reversal" program, insured by the Mutual of Omaha Insurance Company (O'Neill 1993, p. A1).

Consumers participate in a four-part prevention program designed to reverse the effects of heart disease. The four components include diet, moderate exercise, support groups, and meditation.

Q What does a program like this cost?

A In trial programming, the reversal program costs a little more than $3,000 per employee per year, whereas the more traditional approach costs ten times as much (O'Neill 1993, p. A1). Costs are a big factor in the support for this program.

Q Wouldn't the heart reversal program be a complement to our wellness program?

A Absolutely! As a complement to your current wellness program, the heart reversal program would be a good addition. There are also other programs which focus on prevention and health, but not all of them have attained insurance backing. Explore this fine idea with your physician or a certified nurse practitioner.

Q We understand that the best way to prevent large claims and abuse is to get employees to pay a larger share of the costs. Is this true?

A Yes, facts are coming in suggesting a larger deductible and out-of-pocket pay by the consumer—an employee—is a good way to reduce overall costs for claims (Thompson 1992, p. 20).

Q For prevention, what does this suggest?

A These data suggest many consumers are unaware of the actual costs of their health care. There is also a change in attitude. As long as insurance covered a service, consumers did not share the responsibility and therefore the concern in the same way. Reform means the employee as consumer is also getting into prevention. It also suggests that in the future, companies may well need to have more ongoing conversations about costs. A company–family approach to the need to keep costs down is a good prevention strategy.

Q   What are some specific strategies we could use?

A   Some consumers are quite naive about the structure of health care as it is delivered in the twentieth century. Why not have a list of claims for a year, code the identities, and let the employees see how expensive some of those claims are. The frequency of other claims would also be enlightening. This process was used quite successfully with physicians who never worried about treatment and service costs. When these physicians realized the costs of basic medical supplies, they reduced the treatments and supplies they ordered.

Q   What else can we do to involve our employees?

A   Develop an employee consumer board with representatives from a cross-section of your company. Make sure an employee with very high claim use is on the board. The purpose of this board is to get the employees involved in thinking of ways to keep costs down. They can have a positive peer influence on abusers, on high claims, and on employees that complain. In addition, make sure that the link between the costs of the health care and benefits, and the overall profit line for the company, is not overlooked.

Q   We think we have cases of real abuse of our health care benefits. We would like to prevent this in the future. Any ideas?

A   Yes. Let other employees know about high-cost claims. You cannot share the identity of claims or specifics identifying personnel, however, you can list claims in order of costs and frequency.

Q   I think it might be smart to see if there are relationships between some of our claims and certain areas of our employee population. Has this been done?

A   No, but it is an excellent idea. You are bound to see links in terms of demographics such as age or weight of your employee population. Use those data for preventive purposes.

Q   Are there data programs available for prevention planning?

A   No, but a data-entry program such as Paradox or dBase would be quite helpful. Enter all the data from your claims into the system with some accompanying demographic information, code the entries, and apply simple statistics to examine what emerges. Potential relationships are between age and illness, weight and exercise, length of employment and number of claims, and between claim frequency and certain employees.

Q   For preventive purposes and future planning, we would like to see if our health-oriented programming is working. How can we do that?

A   Use a simple data-entry program, enter the data on employees who use the program, and correlate it with their claims data. Keep all the data confidential with codes. Do you see a relationship, for example, between those employees who lose weight and their claims or those who use the jogging program and their claim frequency? This is a starting point.

Q   What if we wanted to be more sophisticated for preventive purposes?

A   Take the next step and examine the correlation between the claim amounts and the cost of the program. This is an excellent way to substantiate the investment in your benefits program.

Q   We want to discuss some trends in health care with our employees but things are changing so fast that we don't even know where they will be in the next century. How can we be fair to our employees and to ourselves in terms of preventing some common problems?

A   Be candid about this with your employees. They know the bottom line is a reality, but they also value their company and their jobs. Let them know something about the complexities of your work. Prevent antagonism in the future by keeping your employees abreast of changes now. Include the rationale for your decision in your information.

Q   The president of our company just faxed us a letter indicating that deductibles will increase for all employees. We are to tell them in one week and implement in the second. How can we prevent this in the future?

A   Gather some data and discuss it with your own boss at the branch. Let him know the impact on the average employee. Request a longer time span in the future. Perhaps the president is unaware of the complexity or the employee sensitivity involved in such decisions.

Q   We want a wise investment in terms of health care for our benefits program in the future. Are the HMOs predicted to increase in number as much as analysts say?

A   If stock indicators are accurate, the big growth will continue in the HMOs of the future (Weber 1993, p. 134). With increasing emphasis on managed-care facilities, the HMO groupings stand a good change of surviving—if not excelling.

Q   We want to cut our health care costs in the future. Where are the biggest cuts coming from?

A   According to reports, the biggest reductions in overall health care costs are incurred by the HMOs of America. In recent times they showed more than a 20 percent reduction in operating costs (Weber 1993, p. 134); not a poor performance at all.

Q   What is the future prediction for the enrollment of HMOs?

A   Whereas HMO enrollment is currently about 43 million people in the U.S., by the turn of the century it is predicted to double to 86 million (Weber 1993, p. 134).

Q   What else can we do to prevent problems in our health care benefits package?

A   One area that many directors of human resources overlook is the resources available to them, such as this book. Newsletters and on-line information via computer networking are other examples. Explore these, although some of them are costly.

Q   If we wanted to really emphasize prevention, what should we do?

A   Get your employees into a health maintenance organization. As part of the HMO Act of 1973, HMOs were required to offer preventive benefits (Piacentini and Foley 1992).

Q   If we want to change in the future and move to prevention what should we consider?

A   Again, give strong consideration to the services in the health maintenance organizations (HMOs) or in the managed-care services. The HMOs, for example, were found to have more offerings in immunizations and inoculations than other types of services (Piacentini and Foley 1992).

Q   What are some of the creative solutions employers are developing to attract and retain employees as a preventive measure? We want to retain a competitive edge over other firms.

A   One good example is a company in Vermont called the Gardeners' Supply which is a $20 million mail-order company (Cronin 1993, p. 31). Their strategy is the development of a health care package which includes the unmarried partners of their employees. As the CEO says, ". . . different lifestyles work here." Others are Lotus Development and International Data Group, both located near or in Boston.

Q   Are there a number of companies moving in this direction?

A   According to recent statistics, few companies currently offer these benefits, but the numbers are increasing daily (Cronin 1993, p. 31). The trend is toward an increase in this benefit.

Q   Are there any data on claims?

A   Yes. Comparison of the claims from married and unmarried partners appear to be similar; no greater for the unmarried (Cronin 1993, p. 31).

Q What is keeping employers from moving into this arena with more enthusiasm?

A There are several issues. Administration is one issue, since employees cannot be treated in the same way for tax purposes. For example, the COBRA laws do not apply to partner benefits. Another is qualifications. Gardeners', a company that recently implemented this benefit, asks for a signed statement of responsibility (Cronin 1993, p. 31).

Q What is the reaction among employees about this newer form of extended coverage?

A According to Gardeners' Supply, when they announced the extended coverage their employees gave them a standing ovation (Cronin 1993, p. 31).

Q If the insurer we use does not cover a partner, what can we do?

A Since many do not cover partners, some use a stipend to cover the employee of an amount similar to a spouse. Partners then find their own coverage with the company financial stipend (Cronin 1993, p. 31).

Q What are employers in the future going to do to prevent drug use on the job?

A A proposed preventive strategy is drug testing on the job. The link between prevention and testing through one's job has been proven successful in several well-placed sources (Lipman 1993, p. 15).

Q What are the figures for drug use at work? Aren't most drug users unemployed?

A Studies suggest that 70 percent of illegal drug users are employed either part- or full-time (Lipman 1993, p. 15).

Q We have thought about drug testing but we are fearful that our workers will resent it. What if we put it into our wellness program as a preventive measure? What would our employee think?

A If your employees are like others they would be in favor of testing. Gallop polls report that between 61 percent and 86 percent of employees are in favor of on-the-job drug testing (Lipman 1993, p. 15). Remember, there are on-the-job injuries and other behaviors related to drugs that employees both fear and resent.

REFERENCES

Cronin, M. 1993. Managing people: Health care for unmarried partners. *INC*, April: 31.

Lipman, I. 1993. Viewpoints: Fight drugs with workplace tests. *New York Times*, 18 July: 15.

1965–1990: 25th anniversary of nurse practitioners. 1990. *Journal of the American Academy of Nurse Practitioners*. 2(3): 93–99.

O'Neill, M. 1993. Unusual heart therapy wins coverage from big insurers. *New York Times*, 28 July: A1.

Piacentini, J., and Foley, J. 1992. *EBRI Databook on Employee Benefits, 2nd ed.* Washington, D.C.: Employee Benefits Research Institute.

Thompson, R. 1992. How to buy health insurance. *Nation's Business*. October: 16–20.

Weher, J. 1993. These days, HMO stocks are in the pink. *Business Week*, 12 July: 134.

13

The Future of Health Care Benefits

Health care is in the forefront of American business. Administrators of health care benefits know that health care reform is changing the administration of benefits as well as the allocation of resources. Employees are aware their health care benefits are changing, including the manner in which the service is delivered and the claim is processed. These changes, both imminent and yet to be revealed, are posing problems that challenge the most creative and resourceful of benefits directors. This chapter addresses these problems. It emphasizes projections for the future and managing the unknown. This chapter provides questions and answers to guide the benefits manager through the uncharted waters.

SAILING IN UNCHARTED WATERS

Q It seems to me we have a difficult time assessing where all this is going. Is this accurate?

A   Although all business is changing rapidly, no sector of the market is changing more rapidly and dramatically than health care. For that reason, the future is unpredictable.

Q   Is there anything in the future of health care that is certain?

A   Indicators suggest continued cost containment is certain. Also, changes in providers and the sites of health care delivery will emerge in a different configuration than in the twentieth century.

Q   What about demographic shifts?

A   These, too, will change, with a continuing trend toward an older population and work force. The needs of this population will differ from those for whom health care programming was designed in the mid-twentieth century.

Q   What are some of the national health care trends human resource directors should pay attention to?

A   Trends to consider include cost relating to reimbursement and payment and the changing structure of the providers. We are moving from a fee-for-service delivery of care to a different structure for the twenty-first century. Although not totally clear, it follows the health maintenance models with more emphasis on groups of providers whether in HMOs or not. There is also an emphasis on variety among those groups of providers with advanced practice nurses and physician assistants working with physicians.

Q   What is vertical integration?

A   There are two main types of integration occurring in health care as it is restructured. *Vertical* is the form in which the aim is to remain cost-effective by spreading the risk of the service across several different forms of the same service.

Therefore, in vertical restructuring, a health service organization, such as an acute-care tertiary hospital, may attempt to meet this aim by purchasing a long-term care facility. It might also purchase a linen supply company to service both the hospital and the long-term facility. As one can see, the services are related or integrated, however, the profits are spread across several services. In the case of the linen supply company, one is slightly different in process stage, albeit related.

Q What is the other main form of integration?

A *Horizontal integration* also targets cost containment and spread of risk, but the method differs. The means is through a monopoly of a similar, if not the same, service in health care. The most common example is a large tertiary hospital which purchases a smaller hospital offering similar services. Monopoly may be attained with one or several purchases.

Q What started integration in health care, or where did it emerge?

A These types of integration were evident in business several decades ago, but they have only recently been utilized in the health care sector. The surge of the restructuring emerged with the introduction of diagnostic related groups or DRGs, which changed the reimbursement of health care payments.

Q Isn't a monopoly a problem within the newer concept of managed competition?

A That is correct. Managed competition attempts to drive costs down or to keep them lowered through natural competition in the market, a phenomenon to which, historically, health care has been particularly immune.

Q Why is it health care does not follow the typical market patterns?

A Mainly, health care does not follow the typical economic analyses because of the difference in supply and demand. The relationship between perceived need and demand is also quite different and controlled by providers, not consumers. Health is probably the most valued commodity, if it can be called a commodity, in the world. The relationship between supply and demand which drives many other forms of business does not apply to health care, mainly due to the nature of the value placed on health care, as well as the ability to obtain access to health care primarily through providers.

Q What about access to health care is different?

A Access to health care is determined, to date, largely by providers. Although a consumer or patient can walk into a hospital, access to medications or certain treatments is controlled; it is not a freely purchased item like other industrial products.

Q Does the fact that consumers do not have final say on or request certain items also affect it?

A Absolutely. An assessment of the problem, called the diagnosis, is completed by a professional who then determines what is appropriate intervention, usually called the treatment. While consumers or patients are increasingly sophisticated about health care and have ideas about their needs and appropriate outcome, outcome or intervention is not, to a very large degree, determined by the consumer. Although the degree of consumer influence has changed dramatically in the latter part of the twentieth century, purchase of health care is still different from the purchase of a dress or tie.

Q How can health care difficulties be anticipated in the future?

A To some extent they cannot. However, if the human resources department sees major changes in the frequency of reimbursed services, this is a strong indicator for attention to certain sectors of the market. Keeping an eye on reimbursement, as well as the claims brought forward by the company, is key to anticipating future problems.

Q Is it anticipated that health care services will still be offered primarily in hospitals?

A Again, nothing is certain. However, trends in the twentieth century suggest that the community services, outpatient-ambulatory facilities, and longer-term facilities are on the increase, an increase that will continue well into the twenty-first century.

Q How important are federal projections for the future?

A Although federal influences are always important, the present climate suggests less emphasis will be placed on federal and more on local, community-oriented, and state-regulated influences. Keep an eye on all, however, especially as disparities emerge.

Q Everyone suggests that acute-care hospitals may be a thing of the past. Is that true?

A No. It will probably mean, however, the hospitals may structure differently. Some of these suggested structure differences are illustrated by the following predictions. It is predicted acute-care hospitals will downsize dramatically, continuing a trend begun in the 1980s and moving into the twenty-first century (Zeller 1993, p. 33). Surveys report that the number of hospitals has declined by more than 9 percent since 1987, but the number of beds has been reactively stable. These figures suggest that the reductions in length of stay are bringing the numbers somewhat in balance.

Q If hospitals are cutting back, what will replace them?

A Experts anticipate an increase in the number of regional or local networks among both physicians and hospitals (Zeller 1993, p. 33).

Q We are a relatively small company with branches throughout one state, most in other small communities. Thus, most of our employees are small-town folks. They are great employees but they are wary of these giant facilities in health care emerging on the horizon. Is this the trend for the future?

A Yes, but they are different from the large organizations or hospitals of the past decades. It is predicted reform and cost containment will result in an increasing number of mergers, acquisitions, or closures of smaller facilities. For better or worse, an increasing number of giant or monolith hospitals is predicted for the future (Zeller 1993, p. 33).

Q The large hospital has always existed. What is different from those projected for the future? Are there differences?

A Yes, there are. One difference is an increasing emphasis on quality as well as cost reduction. This is not to suggest that prior organizations did not offer quality, but there is a heightened awareness of the attention to quality and cost (Zeller 1993, p. 33). Included in projections for the future is an emphasis on results (also called outcomes) of care delivery, an assessment of these results, and the use of these outcomes to confirm quality of care for consumers.

Q   Where does it appear today the future lies in terms of types of plans?

A   Bet on the health maintenance organizations. They have seen enormous growth over the past decade with more expected (Thompson 1993, p. 24).

Q   We are a small company and our employees use a community hospital. What is the prediction for the local community hospital in the future?

A   Although the community hospital saw a large decline in the 1980s of about a 9 percent drop in numbers (Zeller 1993, p. 33), there is the possibility that they may increase, based on the demographic shifts and the shorter stay in acute-care hospitals.

Q   I hear the occupancy rate among hospitals has been fairly steady. Is this true, and if so, why is this?

A   Yes. You are correct. The overall hospital occupancy rate has been hovering at just under 50 percent since 1987 (Zeller 1993, p. 33). The reasons are shorter stays and declining admissions.

Q   While we are trying to keep our costs down, we also see a rise in expenses. What are the projected cost increases in health care benefits?

A   Specific answers are difficult to find. However, based on past increases, the future increase on an annual basis may be as high as 10 percent, until full cost control is in place.

Q   What are the predictions for the future with managed competition. Will it survive?

A   It seems clear that a managed-competition approach will survive. When one examines the main impetus for changes projected for the future, cost reduction is the top priority. Reform suggests a managed approach will not only achieve this outcome but will survive in some form (Flynn and Garland 1993, p. 95).

Q   What are other trends one can forecast?

A   Another trend gathering force is the shift from a production-based economy in health care to a performance-based one (Montague 1993, p. 24).

Q   What indicators suggest the change from production-based, which we have in most of our businesses, to a performance emphasis?

A   One of the leading indicators of change in health care services is the recent emergence of emphasis on what is called outcomes research, or in other words an emphasis on results and research on the results. This emphasis parallels the emphasis on performance of outcomes as indicators of quality of care.

Q   How do physicians view the changes in forms of payment?

A   Although physicians were predominantly paid through fee-for-service structures in the past, they are becoming more enthusiastic about prepaid plans. This is a significant shift in attitude.

Q   It is predicted in the future the real gains will occur in the management of information. How will information management affect our benefits structure?

A   Given the dramatic shifts occurring in the restructuring of health care facilities and their resulting services, there is an increasing need to manage the wealth of information spanning these services. As the patient moves through this restructured system, the information relevant to him or her should follow. This implies a managed information system, affecting the quality of the care as well as the quality of the planning and continuity of the care. While already important, the management of information will be essential in the future.

Q   Several insurers have suggested a key for the future is the management of drugs, or formularies. Is that true?

A   The reshaping of the health care industry has certainly had implications for the drug industry as well as the offering of health care benefits to cover drug prescriptions (Blankenau 1993, p. 36). The formulary, a type of drug dispensary associated with managed-care services, will be a new means of controlling costs for drug services.

Q   I understand the West Coast is moving ahead in some innovative models for health care services. Are there any that could affect us?

A   It is not only the West Coast; there are innovations throughout the states. Since you mention the West, there are several innovations in Oregon, for example, suggesting collaboration, competition, and capitation are in the forefront of health care (Cerne 1993, p. 50).

Q   What does the future hold for primary physicians?

A   As a cost-reduction measure, they are suggested to be the wave of the future (Cerne 1993, p. 50).

Q   What is a fully integrated model? Is it viable in the future?

A   As a form of restructured health care in a *fully integrated model* or structure, all the necessary components are found in a single entity (Hudson 1993, p. 33).

Q   I am concerned in the future we may not have many insurers from which to select our health care benefits. Is this an accurate forecast?

A   Of course, any forecast is subject to change. However, you are also right to assume changes in health care reform will pose more alterations in the insurance industry, potentially reducing the numbers of insurers and increasing their relative size. A smaller number of large insurance companies is predicted (Hudson 1993, p. 33).

Q   What companies are predicted to emerge as the big players in the future of health care insurance so we can think ahead?

A   Again, predictions vary. The major ones, referred to as the "Gang of Five," include Aetna, Cigna, Metropolitan Life, Prudential, and Travelers (Orland 1993, p. 11).

Q   What are the implications for the future of health care benefits if a few larger companies dominate?

A   A major concern for an employer is the range of choice, the ability to negotiate, and the presentation by these larger insurers of a monopsony in economic terms.

Q   Are there other forecasts for large insurer groupings?

A   At least one author suggests these larger companies and groups may encourage more antitrust lawsuits (Orland 1993, p. 11).

Q Given the potential for larger insurers and a monopsony developing among the health care insurance industry, what protection is there in place to prevent abuse?

A Those dimensions are yet to be developed. However, the federal government, as well as consumer groups are aware of the potential for abuse.

Q Given the changes in the facilities offering health care, what should companies watch out for as companies continue to offer health care benefits?

A In terms of the actual service, one would want to inquire about the range of services and the quality. In terms of the restructuring of facilities, inquire about the continuity of care and the planning of care, especially discharge planning and return of the employees to their original communities. These are particularly problematic in new systems.

Q As a resource director, I am aware studies have found that the poor population is, generally speaking, a less healthy population. Does it suggest we should, in the future, differentially project health care benefits to try to keep the lower-paid employees more healthy and perhaps reduce the amount given to the more highly reimbursed employees?

A It is an interesting question. According to studies reported in the *New England Journal of Medicine* (Herring 1993, p. 2), there is little question the rich get healthier. However, the findings of these studies indicate that the difference has to do with the use of health-oriented information.

Q Are there programs or trends suggested by these studies we could use for future benefits programs?

A Certainly. The study found the richer tended to take better care of themselves; they quit smoking, ate better, and exercised. You could reward these behaviors in future benefits programming.

Q Our employees are concerned that they will have limited insurance in the future. They say a lot of folks are uninsured. Do analysts agree?

A Probably not, although there will certainly be changes. If one looks at current statistics, a little under 17 percent of all workers have no insurance in the U.S. (Eckholm 1993, p. 5). Access for all, however, is in the forefront of reform.

Q Are there some groups who tend to require more insurance than others; will this stay the same in the future?

A It is hard to predict how groups will shift in the future. However, based on the current facts, there are differences among groups or types of workers.

Q Our company is in the construction business. We will probably change the benefits package we offer in the future by decreasing our current offerings, but it seems many of my colleagues in the construction industry are not offering any health insurance to their construction employees. Is that predicted to stay the same in the future?

A The construction industry is one in which the number of uninsured workers is above average. For example, compared to a national average of 17 percent, your industry is hovering around 30 percent (Eckholm 1993, p. 5). There are no predictions for a reduction in the proportion.

Q I think the average worker in our company is more concerned with the security of his or her health care than anything else. What does the future predict for security of health care?

A   You are right on target with the issues of security. Health care reform is based on the concept of security for all workers as its main thrust. For some, health care security is also referred to as access to health care for all; care that cannot be removed or lost.

Q   If the country moves into more managed care, doesn't it make sense to go ahead with some coverage claim items now?

A   Absolutely. If you have an elective surgery pending, for example, that is out of the mainstream but is currently covered, the chances of its being covered in the future are less likely.

Q   What are the implications of this situation for our employees?

A   If an employee wants surgery or treatment done, then go ahead now while it is covered. This is not to suggest you encourage a lot of treatments, but if the employees want it anyway, perhaps better now than later, which may mean never.

Q   If we want to invest in the future for our own growth and planning, where is the wise investment?

A   If you are planning a change, with the current emphasis on the managed-care facilities and health care delivery, I would bet on the HMO types of offerings and their variants.

Q   We have been hearing a lot about the health maintenance organizations. However, we are a public utility. We would want to go with a publicly traded HMO. What is their prediction for the future and is it as good as the private HMOs?

A   The publicly traded HMOs are showing growth as are the privates. The publicly traded are accounting for over one-third of the U.S. enrollers (Weber 1993, p. 134).

Q   What are the predictions for technology and information management vis-à-vis health care benefits?

A   There are a few but they are consistent. Data and information management will be bywords. It is possible, for example, that an employee will obtain a service, file a claim, and receive action without ever filling out a form. Advances in this field will make the exchange of information easier.

Q   What are some implications for the director of human resources?

A   Your job should show a reduction in paperwork with an increase in documentation and data retrieval. Data will be at your fingertips but will require analysis. Familiarize yourself with computer statistical analysis and data management.

Q   Is it true that flexible benefits plans will be obsolete in the future?

A   Quite possibly (Foster 1986). The advantage of the flexible benefits plan is the tax-free feature for reimbursement of health care costs employees pay out-of-pocket. That aspect will probably not survive. The jury is still out on whether other flex aspects will remain; perhaps they will in an altered form.

Q   If a flex plan is to survive, what is the best bet on what will make it?

A   Among those moving well into the twenty-first century will be forms that are based not on pretax dollars, but on the after-tax amount (Foster 1986).

Q   Where are the initiatives occurring in the use of alliances?

A   California was the first state to move ahead with an alliance from which small companies, those with between five and 50 employees, could purchase standard and discounted plans from participating insurers (Thompson 1993, p. 24).

Q   Right now we use a form of self-insurance in which we basically pay for health care and claims of our ten employees out-of-pocket. Will we be able to continue this procedure in the future?

A   Probably not, although there is no consensus (Thompson 1993, p. 24). However, with the recent reform changes the self-insurance dimension is deemed obsolete.

Q   Is it true that directors of human resources will need more statistical and data management skills in the future? What kind in particular?

A   Absolutely, but then everything in the future speaks to computers and their technology; the same is true of the benefits management section of companies. In particular, learn a basic data management program such as dBase, word processing, and a statistical analysis program like SPSS-X; learn how to do fundamental statistics and analyses with these.

Q In terms of family leaves for employees in the future, will the leave segment of the package change?

A What will change will be the demographic shifts we now see in society with more emphasis on leaves for the elderly at home or spouses, rather than for children. The leave was originally designed for parents and children and then expanded. One implication for the benefits program is that reasons for taking leaves will not have resolutions for them the way many do today; they may be prolonged or chronic health situations.

Q As the major insurers move away from an indemnity service of the past, what does it mean for the future of hospitals? We use our local hospital a lot and feel it is good to our employees.

A If the hospital can negotiate with the insurers for a reduced fee, then the local hospital will probably survive and do well. The key is the network or affiliation between the hospital and the insurer. These arrangements are now out in the open under networks, alliances, and managed care.

Q When people leave the indemnity services, where do they tend to go? We are assessing a change in our own employees.

A When companies switch from the traditional services of insurance they used in the past, they typically go to a managed-care program like an HMO.

Q One of the concerns I have is with the dramatic changes in acuity levels among hospitalized patients and the reduced length of stay. I see our employees coming back to work too early; they stay sick longer but are working. Will this situation get worse in the future?

A   Predictions vary, however, cost containment is here to stay. What will change is the location of the hospital stay with less reliance on the acute-care sites which have traditionally been hospitals and more on the community-based facilities. Encourage the employee to take care of him- or herself and to enhance health and emphasize prevention. Remember, in today's market economy employees are also worried about their jobs.

Q   What will health care sites look like for our future employees?

A   They will be networks of restructured facilities moving the patient—your employee—from the community, into the treatment setting, through discharge planning, and back into the community for longer-term care with home services. Needs will drive care facilities but they will look different by the turn of the century.

Q   We use a rural site for some of our care. We like the service and our employees are especially fond of the nurses and physicians. The service is quality and caring. Will these sorts of services be available in the future?

A   Although rural and smaller facilities are expected to continue to provide care, your employees will probably find themselves a part of a larger system, alliance, or certainly a network which includes larger and smaller facilities. Information technology will link these together so the rural system will not seem remote; communication and technology links will be needed to compete in new markets. At best, it will retain its caring and quality features for your employees.

Q   I worry my job as a director of human resources will change dramatically. With massive downsizing in the health care field and cuts in middle management, maybe the office will only need one person and employees. Is this true?

A There will undoubtedly be changes in the benefits office, primarily driven by the turbulent health care environment. However, there will always be a need for a sensitive individual to interpret the complex and ever-changing health care system that affects our employees.

Q What are the driving forces that will affect health care benefits in the future?

A The changing demographics as well as changing family characteristics, will have an enormous impact on the shape of health care benefits (Stelluto and Klein 1990, p. 38).

Q What are some of the changes that directors could anticipate in health care benefits?

A Basically, they will need to be much more flexible and responsive to the employee (Stelluto and Klein 1990, p. 38). There will be less demarcation between the actual pay or remuneration of employees and their benefits. The issue will be reward for work, with less distinction between reward and work.

Q What about the increasing numbers of employees with substance abuse problems? Will that continue?

A Alas, it appears that this will continue. More emphasis will be given to addressing substance abuse in the workplace. For example, in 1990, substance abuse in all forms cost the U.S. $229 billion (U.S. Department of Labor 1992a, p. 3).

Q Will there be more emphasis on abuse programming as a health care benefit?

A   Yes. In addition to the real cost, the hidden cost in lost productivity among workers was over $100 billion per year in the early 1990s. One can also understand why, between 1983 and 1989, benefits programs to cover substance abuse went from 50 percent of all full-time employees to nearly 90 percent. This will become commonplace in benefits programs.

Q   Is it true the focus on wellness and health will predominate in the future?

A   They will surely be an important component of any benefits package, since there is an increasing amount of emphasis placed on both of these types of programs.

Q   What indicators are there now of these changes?

A   An alternative nontraditional program called a "heart reversal" program including diet, moderate exercise, meditation, and support groups, qualified for insurance reimbursement in 1993 (O'Neill 1993, p. A1). This program is carried by Mutual of Omaha Insurance Company with possible coverage being explored by Blue Cross and Blue Shield Companies in several states. Others will undoubtedly follow this first reimbursement of a major preventive and nontraditional program for heart disease.

Q   Will the components of a wellness program change dramatically in the future?

A   Probably not as dramatically as the inclusion of employees in these programs. It will change with the results of new research or findings that link wellness with productivity or prevention. These can, of course, be dramatic.

Q   What will be the greatest emphasis in the future?

A   The greatest emphasis will be on the containment of medical costs and, as a link to those, prevention of problems. Remember as an index medical care costs went from 92.5 to 162.8 between 1982 and 1990, whereas the consumer price index went from 96.5 to 130.7 (U.S. Department of Labor 1992b, p. 9).

Q   What can we expect in the future for the amount companies will be paying for retiree health care benefits?

A   According to government reports, by the year 2008 annual costs will reach approximately $22 billion using current dollars (U.S. Department of Labor 1992b, p. 9).

Q   What is the current projection for the unfunded amount for retirees?

A   Currently, the unfunded amount is about $227 billion. That estimate is a major reason for including unfunded accounts in projections as a liability.

Q   Given these rising costs and the enormous amount of future projected amounts, what do you think companies will do to reduce these costs, or to keep them in check?

A   Several measures are suggested. One is to require retirees to pay more into the fund, to limit their medical services, or to limit coverage to fewer retirees (McNamee, Weber, and Mitchell 1993, p. 114).

Q   Do we have to cover retirees for health care benefits in the future?

A   It is hard to tell, however, current emphasis in health care reform on health care security and access to care by all workers suggests it might. Current laws address pensions but not specifically health care (McNamee, Weber, and Mitchell 1993, p. 114).

Q Are there precedents for reductions?

A Yes. Studies confirm companies offering health care may reduce coverage.

Q If there are no legal mandates to include health care, isn't it logical that companies will increasingly drop retiree health care since it comes up as a liability?

A It is logical because elimination would reduce liability, thereby creating a more favorable financial picture of the company (McNamee, Weber, and Mitchell 1993, p. 115). It would be a more positive financial picture than the retiree benefits posted as a liability.

Q Does this seem to be what might happen in the future?

A Yes, but only from a bottom-line perspective. From the view of the employee and the image of the company the answer may be different. Remember there is more emphasis on employer-and-employee relations in the reform era, as well as universal access to health care.

REFERENCES

Blakenau, R. 1993. Confused consumers. *Hospitals & Health Networks*, 5 July: 36.

Cerne, F. 1993. Networking: Portland, Oregon. *Hospitals & Health Networks*, 5 July: 50.

Eckolm, E. 1993. The uninsured: 37 million and growing. *New York Times*, 11 July: p. 5.

Flynn, J., and Garland, S. 1993. Final option: Radical surgery. *Business Week*, 11 January: 95.

Foster, R. 1986. *The Manager's Guide to Employee Benefits*. New York: Facts on File.

Herring, H. 1993. Business diary. *New York Times*, 11 July: 2.

Hudson, R. 1993. Three major models. *Hospitals & Health Networks*, 20 June: 33.

McNamee, M., Weber, J., and Mitchell, R. Health-care reform: It's already here. *Business Week*, 14 June: 114–21.

Montague, J. 1993. Special report: Straight talk. *Hospitals & Health Networks*, 5 July: 24.

O'Neill, M. 1993. Unusual heart therapy wins coverage from big insurers. *New York Times*, 28 July: A1.

Orland, L. 1993. Health reform runs antitrust risk. *New York Times*, 11 July: 11.

Stelluto, G., and Klein, D. 1990. Compensation trends into the 21st century. *Monthly Labor Review*, February: 38–40.

Thompson, R. 1993. Health-reform watch. *Nation's Business*, July: 24–25.

U.S. Department of Labor. 1992b. *Employee Benefits in a Changing Economy*, 2394, September: 1–18.

U.S. Department of Labor. 1992a. *Substance Abuse Provisions in Employee Benefit Plans*, 2412, August: 1–13.

Weher, J. 1993. These days HMO stocks are in the pink. *Business Week*, 12 July: 134.

Zeller, W., and McNamee, M. 1993. And now, monolith hospitals. *Business Week*, 28 June: 33.

Index